CAREER COACH

HOW TO PLAN YOUR CAREER AND LAND YOUR PERFECT JOB

Withdrawn From Stock
Dublin City Public Libraries

Corinne Mills
Personal Career Management

Leabharlanna Poibli Chathair Bhaile Átha Cliath
Dublin City Public Libraries

D0673660

Career Coach: How to plan your career and land your perfect job

This second edition published in 2017 by Trotman Publishing, a division of Crimson Publishing Ltd, 19-21c Charles Street, Bath, BA1 1HX

© Crimson Publishing Ltd 2017

Author Corinne Mills

British Library Cataloguing in Publication Data
A catalogue record for this book is available from the British Library

ISBN 978 1 84455 641 0

All rights reserved. No part of this publication may be reproduced, stored in a retrieval system or transmitted in any form or by any means, electronic and mechanical, photocopying, recording or otherwise without prior permission of Crimson Publishing Ltd.

Typeset by IDSUK (DataConnection) Ltd
Printed and bound in Malta by Gutenberg Press, Ltd

CONTENTS

TABLE OF EXERCISES

ABOUT THE AUTHOR

This book is about you, your career journey and achieving your career goals. However, as I'm going to be your personal career coach and guide throughout this book, let me introduce myself.

I'm Corinne Mills, Managing Director of the UK's leading career coaching and outplacement company, Personal Career Management (www.personalcareermanagement.com) which I founded in 2003. My own career background includes over 20 years' experience in career management working with thousands of individuals ranging from CEOs to those looking for their very first proper job. They've all had their own unique career challenges and experiences and I've loved being able to help them flourish professionally.

Before working in career management I held senior-level roles in Human Resources in which I was responsible for all aspects of people management including hiring and firing, staff performance and learning and development. This nitty-gritty knowledge of how organisations really work has always been a distinct advantage when it comes to advising my coaching clients on career tactics.

My earlier career was somewhat different. Until the age of 26 I worked as an actress and was an occasional singer in a new wave band. While it was great fun, it was also a precarious way to earn a living. Armed with an English and drama degree but with limited experience of anything else, I had countless rejections before finally landing a job as a trainee personnel officer. I worked hard and rose through the HR corporate ranks, studying at night for my MA in Human Resource Management and later becoming a Fellow of the Chartered Institute of Personnel and Development (CIPD) and chair of a CIPD branch.

inspired way to bring Corinne's tried and tested model to you direct so that you can access and work on your own career in your own time. Corinne has been able to share her many years of career coaching within the format of a user-friendly book, bringing her career management expertise and experience to a wider audience.

Career Coach is more than a career workbook. As important as the resources within the book, is that you will have Corinne alongside you as your own personal career coach. There is a real sense of her presence while working through the book as you consider your own career story and make plans for your career ahead. I hope that you too will experience the warmth, understanding and energy that Corinne offers her clients.

I wish you well on your journey together.

Janet Sheath
Teaching Fellow, Birkbeck College, University of London
Member of the Institute of Career Guidance

ACKNOWLEDGEMENTS

To Jonathan, thank you for your love, sense of humour and fearlessness.

Elliot and Louis – thank you for your patience while I've been writing this book. Whatever you both grow up to be, I hope that your life and career will be fulfilling.

Thank you to Janet Sheath who has been my touchstone in my career management work. Her advice and mentoring has been invaluable and inspiring. I feel privileged to have been able to work with her.

I also want to say thank you to the Personal Career Management team; it's great to work with such a talented, knowledgeable and good-hearted group of people.

Thank you also to the many clients I have worked with over the years; it's been hugely enjoyable and challenging and I have learnt so much from you.

Finally, thanks also to Della Oliver and the team at Trotman Publishing for their continued encouragement and patience.

ABOUT THIS BOOK

Are you ready for your next career move? Have you reached the top of your career ladder and are unsure what to do next? Perhaps you are looking for a career change or a new challenge. Or maybe you've seen friends fast-track their career and want to accelerate your career too.

There may be many different reasons that have led you to read this book. These could include:

- seeking a role with more responsibility, pay or development opportunities
- wanting to move from a job that you are not currently enjoying
- feeling stuck and not knowing what you want next career-wise
- looking for a change in career direction or a different way of working
- wanting a better quality of life or work/life balance.

You may have been thinking about these things for a while or perhaps something has happened recently, either at work or in your personal life, which has given your career management a new sense of urgency.

Whatever your current career situation, this book is going to change your career prospects!

How is it going to do this? Well, there is no magic wand, but there is a formula. It's called personal career coaching. It will help you look objectively at your career so that you can make smart, realistic decisions regarding your next career move and turn any career aspirations from wishful thinking into reality.

I have been using career coaching for many years in my company Personal Career Management, helping thousands of individuals to successfully progress their career.

Career coaching is based on a combination of well researched and sometimes complex career and psychological theory as well as practical knowledge about the job market. This has meant that until now, if you wanted career coaching, you had to go to a specialist.

However, the aim of this book is to open up a new, user-friendly route to career coaching, making it accessible for anyone who wants to pro-actively manage their career.

How this book works

We'll start by helping you understand your current career situation and how you got there. You'll learn how to assess your 'career capital', so you can see what you have to offer prospective employers and how you benchmark with other candidates. We'll look at how to explore your options and make good career decisions that will work for you. Then we'll turn to the practicalities to create a career action plan. There will be lots of advice on how to impress recruitment decision-makers and tackle common career challenges including insights from individuals who have made positive changes in their own career about what worked for them. By the end of the book we will have captured all your thoughts and research together to help you create a 'Career Insights' document that will be your personal roadmap for managing your career for the future.

As with anything in life, the more you put into this book, the more you'll get out of it. Some exercises you will find easier than others, but every one of them is worth doing, and I recommend working through them in order, without missing any out. The exercises work best when you can immerse yourself in some deep thinking, reflection and research in a quiet, undisturbed space. Sample answers are provided for all of the exercises to give you some guidance but your response is always going to be very individual to you. Feel free to ask people you trust for input on the exercises too as they can often have useful insights that you may have missed.

At the end of Parts 1 to 5 of the book, there is a 'reflections' exercise for you to write down any ideas, key points, thoughts or questions that have emerged so far. It's a way to chart your progress in the career coaching process, capture your learning and note down anything that strikes you as significant, including actions to be taken. These will be especially helpful to review when you come to write your career summary in Part 9.

You'll see that some of the exercises are marked with the symbol and this indicates that the exercise is downloadable from our website at www.personalcareermanagement.com/careercoach. This is especially helpful if you need more room to write your answers than is available in the book.

Let's start!

Understanding your current career situation

We are going to start the career coaching process by conducting a very thorough career diagnosis. Your career is multi-layered and it's helpful to poke beneath the layers if you really want to understand what is going on. It's an important first stage because very often individuals focus too narrowly on what they see as their immediate career issue and make assumptions about the solutions, rather than seeing the bigger picture.

We will start by looking broadly at your current career situation and then examine it in more detail from a number of different perspectives.

In this section we will:

■ complete a career health check

■ draw a picture of your world

■ explore your life/work balance

■ identify your priorities for change

Do you know what role you would like next? If so, what is it?

Are there any threats to your current role, for example redundancy?

How employable do you think you are – and how have you tested this?

Are there any other factors that might influence your career?

EXAMPLE

On a Monday morning, how do you feel about the prospect of going into work?

I have a sick feeling in my stomach on the train going in. It's not so bad when I'm there, but I hate the thought of going in.

Which aspects of your work do you like or are of interest to you?

I like working with the customers, helping them find solutions to their queries and acting as an intermediary; I have good relationships with them and it feels good if I can sort out their problems for them.

What aspects of your work are the least enjoyable?

My boss tends to micro-manage and want things done in a particular way which I think sometimes is a waste of time. Don't always feel valued. Sometimes feel I am being de-skilled because not allowed to use my initiative.

What have your relationships with your manager and colleagues been like?

Generally supportive but I don't think they realise just how much I do for the company on the customer side and not sure if anyone else could do that side of my job as well.

Has your work situation affected life outside work?

I don't mind talking to customers at weekends if it keeps them happy, although it can be a bit of a pain sometimes.

When you talk about your work to others, are you positive or negative?

Very negative. I do feel unappreciated and annoyed that others seem to be favourites and I am getting overlooked.

What do friends and family think of your career situation?

They think I am being sidelined and they know I feel quite stressed.

What would you like to change about your current job/career situation?

More trust from my boss and greater freedom in the way I get things done.

Do you know what role you would like next? If so, what is it?

Want promotion within my current company or, failing that, elsewhere.

Are there any threats to your current role, for example redundancy?

Potential threat of redundancy.

How employable do you think you are – and how have you tested this?

I think I am very employable but I haven't had much success with my applications for jobs.

Are there any other factors that might influence your career?

The company is restructuring at work so there is a potential threat that staff numbers may be reduced in the department.

Chris

Now that we have completed this initial career health check and gained an overview of your current career situation, let's explore a little further and a little deeper …

2 YOUR WORLD

You are unique and so is your view of the world and your career. Your subjectivity is perfectly natural and likely to be influenced by many things, including your current state of mind, your upbringing, cultural factors, self-expectations and your life experiences to date.

For instance, you may find your job boring, while your colleague, in a similar job, loves theirs. You might find the travel into work straightforward whereas others would hate it. You may be reluctant to push yourself forward for a promotion opportunity when it arises, while a less talented peer has no such hesitation.

There are many occasions when this subjectivity will serve us well, for example helping us to endure tough times because we have a strong belief that something better is around the corner.

However, it can also sometimes put stumbling blocks in our way perhaps leading us to underestimate our capabilities, to feel things are hopeless or to misread the needs or intentions of others. This is particularly true in career situations that are emotionally sensitive as we can lose objectivity when we are trying to psychologically protect ourselves.

In this chapter, we are going to look much more deeply at your subjective world because, whether you are aware of it or not, your perceptions about your career will be shaping your reality. They filter the information you take in and influence your behaviour and career decisions. Where emotion is involved, your perceptions may be skewed even further than usual.

So to help you understand your inner landscape a little more, complete the following exercise to go deeper into your world.

PICTURE YOUR WORLD

1. You are going to draw a picture of your world. It is not meant to be a realistic picture but a personal one: your drawing ability is the least important part of this exercise.

2. Your drawing could be lifelike, abstract or in the form of a diagram. It could include physical things, such as people or places, as well as more intangible elements such as emotions, events or metaphors. You might want to use colour to make it come alive and boost your creativity.

3. There are no rules about what you should include in your drawing, but some suggestions are:
   - your key challenges, e.g. strong/difficult relationships at work
   - any issues you feel you are wrestling with, such as career indecision or inner conflicts
   - significant people, including family members, friends, colleagues and role models
   - your health and well-being, e.g. stress or anxiety
   - your commitments and priorities, e.g. money and family life
   - your social life and activities outside of work, including hobbies and community work.

TIP

Find a way to represent in your picture any emotions you feel.

4. Be as spontaneous as possible and include anything that comes into your head – even if it seems relatively minor in the scheme of things. Enjoy being creative and expressive. You are the only one who needs to understand your picture, so don't worry about how it looks.

5. Take a minimum of 20 minutes to do your drawing, and keep it for reference.

6. There is an example on page 9 that you can use for inspiration.

7. Once you have finished your drawing, take a moment to look at the whole picture and think about what it is telling you. Now answer the questions below.

What key elements did you choose to include in your picture and why?

Are there any important elements missing from the picture that you have forgotten or perhaps taken for granted?

What are the positive aspects of your picture?

Did your picture show any areas of conflict or tension?

What emotions surfaced during this exercise or are represented in the picture, e.g. pride, frustration?

Is there anything better you could do right now that would change your picture for the better?

Did anything else come out of this exercise for you?

My world picture

My world picture

What key elements did you choose to include in your picture and why?

Me running around all over the place because it feels like I am always in a rush. Included image of me gardening because I feel that things that I enjoy and need to do at home are neglected because I don't have time. Love doing the bedtime stories with the kids but am often half asleep so not giving them the attention they deserve.

Are there any important elements missing from the picture that you have forgotten or perhaps taken for granted?

My ex-partner – noticeable by their absence. Haven't included any friends or social life but perhaps that is because it feels non-existent at the moment. Although friends have been a great source of support to me.

What are the positive aspects of your picture?

The kids are good. The fact that I do have my mum to help. The fact that I have a job.

Did your picture show any areas of conflict or tension?

The stress of always rushing across town to be somewhere – always worried about being late. Difficult relationship with my mum but feels like everything would fall apart if I didn't have her to rely on. Never feeling like I have any personal down time.

What emotions surfaced during this exercise or are represented in the picture, e.g. pride, frustration?

Exhaustion seemed to be the main emotion. Feeling tired from running around everywhere. Feeling guilty about the kids and frustrated by my mum who is really good at looking after the kids after school but is often quite critical of me and can be insensitive.

Is there anything you could do right now that would change your picture for the better?

Talk to my boss about more flexible working. Look for a new job that could offer this.

Did anything else come out of this exercise for you?

I feel cornered. I know what I should do but it requires more energy than I have at the moment and that is making me feel very frustrated, both with myself and my circumstances.

Lara

How did you find this exercise? Did you get really involved in drawing the picture? Were you able to express how you feel about things right now? If you didn't, try the exercise again, this time giving yourself permission to really engage with it. You need to do this with all the exercises in the book to get maximum benefit.

Viewing your world

Let's look more closely at what you've drawn, and why.

Our pictures serve as a very useful psychological snapshot of where we are now. They capture what we see as the key elements in our lives and illustrate any problems or tensions, the depths of our emotions and how they relate to other aspects of our lives.

> *I was standing in treacle – stuck, weighted down, messy. Whereas everyone else around me was whizzing around. Everyone else seemed to be fine but I felt unimportant, stuck, ignored.*
>
> **David**

For instance, many of my clients have drawn pictures that express the challenges which brought them to career coaching. Their pictures can be dominated by question marks, crossroads or the see-saw of work/life balance. In one client's picture there was a huge vacuum cleaner as the central symbol, representing the individual's feeling of being overwhelmed by the challenge of holding down a job and family commitments. Hoovering wasn't the most important thing in her life – but what it represented for her was very powerful indeed.

If elements of your picture seem disproportionately large, this may reflect just how much time you are spending thinking, worrying or dealing with this particular element.

Because your picture is a subjective one, interpreting it is very personal. Only you really know why you chose to include some items and not others and why you represented them in the way you have. This exercise is simply a reflection of some of the conscious and subconscious thoughts that may feel very intense for you right now.

Understanding your emotional landscape is an essential part of the career coaching process because managing your career can be challenging psychologically. Your emotions can be a great motivator to propel you into action. However, they can also sometimes make things more difficult than they need to be, especially if you need to do things outside your comfort zone such as take risks or ditch your natural modesty to convince an employer that they should hire you.

This chapter was designed to raise awareness of the emotional forces at work. Make a note of those that you are affected by; you are likely to find that they will pop up again as you continue your career coaching journey through this book. We'll also be looking at this in Part 6 where there will be advice on strategies that you can use to manage your emotions and challenge any unhelpful subjectivity during a period of career transition.

> *My picture reflected back to me how little confidence I had in my own abilities. It was full of self-doubt – even though I had a really good appraisal this year. I didn't include any of the people who were supportive to me and just focused on the negative people. Why did I do that?*
>
> **Angela**

3 WORK/LIFE BALANCE

Now we are going to move to another vantage point from which to view your current situation – the relationship between your work and the rest of your life.

Although our work is an important part of our sense of identity, you are so much more than your job title. You have other roles, responsibilities and interests, for example as a friend, partner, parent, carer, citizen or in pursuing hobbies or community causes that are close to your heart.

You may have career ambitions but you have life needs and aspirations too. These may be about having a loving relationship, a great social life, moving house, raising happy children, making a difference to the world or anything else that is fundamental to your sense of self and life's purpose.

> Thirty-eight per cent of employees surveyed said they are under excessive pressure at work at least once a week. A third of employees (33%) say they come home from work exhausted either often (24%) or always (9%). Public sector employees are significantly more likely than private sector employees to say that they come home from work exhausted.
>
> **CIPD Employee Outlook Report, Autumn 2016**

Getting the balance right

Ideally your life goals and needs will work in a complementary way with your career but there are often tensions. Some of these may even have been revealed when you completed Exercise 2.

Work/life balance always needs careful monitoring because workplaces are high-pressure environments and it's rarely possible to get to the bottom of your to-do list at the end of a day. Technology that allows us to work from home also makes it far more difficult to disconnect from work because every time we turn on our phone we may see work emails coming in. Even if we are not physically working, we may be thinking about work.

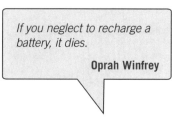

> *If you neglect to recharge a battery, it dies.*
>
> **Oprah Winfrey**

Sometimes this means we have to make minor or temporary compromises. You may need to occasionally work late to complete a project, meet a tough deadline or deal with an emergency. Your job may involve frequent travelling or weekend work, but if you and your family are happy to accept this, it isn't in itself necessarily problematic.

> *It was when I realised I only had suits for work and jogging bottoms for around the house that it hit me that I never do anything outside of work.*
>
> **Karen**

However, if you currently feel overwhelmed or resentful about the long hours you need to work or if it's having a destructive impact on other aspects of your life, then it's definitely time to reassess your commitments.

Thinking about your balance

Work/life balance is a very common issue individuals bring to career coaching. They may be struggling with an unreasonable workload or have reached a time in their life when they want a different type of balance.

Sometimes the solution is to find another job, or, on occasion, another profession. For instance, some management consultancies will expect you to accept assignments away from home and work long hours on time-critical projects. While there may be some room for manoeuvure, you might need to accept that if these are the job requirements you either need to tolerate them or leave.

> *I had a difficult customer who would regularly ring me at weekends just to whinge. It would really wind me up. Then one day I'd just had enough and told her that I wouldn't be available to take her calls at the weekend. She still tried it, but I let it go to voicemail. She is still pretty unpleasant but I only have to put up with her during the week now. I should have laid down ground rules at the start.*
>
> **Aman**

> My boss is sending me emails at all times of the day and night. Do I have to become a workaholic insomniac too?
>
> **Paul**

However, it is also worth considering whether you are in any way contributing to a blurring of a healthy work/life boundary.

I've worked with several clients who came to career coaching in a desperate state because they felt their employer was expecting them to work all hours. One typical example included a manager who felt 'burnt out'. She would work late and come in very early in the morning in order to clear the backlog. Did her organisation really require her to work all these hours? No, they didn't. Would it have been acceptable to have some backlog? Yes. Unless they were going to employ an additional person, some backlog would be inevitable. Had she ever raised this as an issue with her employer? No. It transpired that there had been a similar pattern in her last three jobs. As we dug deeper, it emerged that her work/life imbalance was less to do with her employer who was in fact very supportive towards her, and more to do with her low self-esteem as she felt compelled to work long hours to show how indispensable she was. Her exhaustion understandably had a negative effect on her performance and strained relationships which she then tried to compensate for by working even longer hours. She would take the same problem with her to every job unless she learned how to redraw her own work/life boundaries.

During 2015/16 there were 488,000 cases of work-related stress with 11.7 million working days lost. The main work factors cited as the cause were workload pressures, tight deadlines, too much responsibility and a lack of managerial support.

UK Health and Safety Executive

This is not to say that unreasonable bosses don't exist, nor organisations with a culture of long working hours, because of course they do. But if you are someone who is feeling the stress of working long hours, then it is also your responsibility to manage this. Stress and tiredness can impair your judgement and cognitive abilities so that you start making mistakes and may fall ill.

It may be far better to finish off work at a reasonable time and then attack the work with gusto the next morning when you are feeling rested. If the workload is really unmanageable you must talk to your manager. Ask them to decide which of your tasks are priorities and which can wait. Request an extended deadline or additional support. Unless you tell them there is a problem, they won't know until you fail to deliver, and that's never the best time to be having a conversation with your manager.

Improving the balance

Most people find it tricky to some extent to balance their work and personal life, but there are lots of things that you can do to improve your work/life balance.

Consider the different personal aspects of your life as outlined in the headings below and then complete Exercise 3 on page 17. The exercise will help flush out any work/life conflicts that need addressing and provide some suggestions for improvement.

Family

Do you feel that you have quality time with the family? This might include having fun weekends together, being able to help the kids with their homework, caring for an aged parent or simply visiting family members.

Personal relationships

On the romantic front, are things as you would wish them to be? Are there other relationships that need attention?

Finances

Everyone would like more money, but do you have financial problems? If so, what are the risks and what do you need to do about the situation?

Fun

What is your social life like? Do you have sufficient down time outside work? Do you have fun times when you can just enjoy yourself and recharge your batteries?

Personal growth

Are you as intellectually, spiritually or even physically stretched as you would wish to be? Are you interested in learning and development, self-help literature or the arts? Do you follow a faith? Do you enjoy physical challenges such as training for marathons or learning to dance?

Community

Do you have community responsibilities that are important to you? For instance, volunteering for a charity, supporting a political party, sitting on the PTA or residents' association. Are you as involved in your community as you would like to be?

Health and well-being

Have you any health concerns? Do you feel good about yourself? Are there concerns about the health and well-being of any of the people who are close to you?

Other personal needs

Is there anything else going on in your life that is causing tensions or needs attention?

EXERCISE 3

WORK/LIFE BALANCE ASSESSMENT

1. Consider the following for each of the headings below:
   What is working well?
   What needs improvement and how could you bring this about?
   What impact, if any, does it have on your working life or vice versa?
2. Add other headings if there are other aspects of your life you feel need attention.
3. You'll find an example on page 18.

Family

Personal relationships

Finances

Fun

Personal growth

Community

Health and well-being

Other personal needs

EXAMPLE

Family

Kids are doing fine at school. Wife is enjoying her new job. Mum is going to need more help in the future. Work have been understanding about mum but it does take time looking after her.

Personal relationships

Happily married. Don't go out much. When I work late it does cause arguments because we both get ratty. Should start to minimise late working at the office and start to go out more at the weekend and even maybe midweek go for a drink together or to the cinema.

Finances

I have a job so income coming in but having to dig into savings. No pay rise at work for two years yet everything going up in price. Need to do something to increase income. Ask boss for a pay rise? I need a better-paid job, but should I also look to reduce outgoings?

Fun

When we go out we do have a good time together. Weekends often spent on routine stuff – not enough fun. Work can be very stressful so need to let off some steam at weekends and chill out otherwise work would feel just overwhelming. Should start inviting friends over. Organise some weekend breaks.

Personal growth

Really enjoyed my management course. Learned a lot. Feel I've got lots more to learn. I'm using the knowledge in current role but definitely good for the next step up. I should find the time to read more books on leadership and see if more courses available. Ask HR for what they would recommend.

Community

Got involved with the Fun Run which was good. Feel bad that I am not doing anything with the kids' schools. There are initiatives at work to encourage employees to get involved with their local communities but I haven't really done anything about that yet. Could help out with the Scouts when they need 'dad' help.

Health and well-being

Lost half a stone in weight with recent flu. Do feel very stressed. Seem to have constant colds and flu, so not 100%. Need to go back to gym – maybe have a health check and watch the wine intake.

Other personal needs

Want to help my son prepare for his exams as I know he is struggling a bit. Maybe I should do an MBA. Would love to travel to China.

Stephen

How to leave work on time

Give yourself a reason to leave the office on time

Sometimes it's easier for parents to avoid presenteeism, as they at least have the excuse of needing to pick up their kids. If it helps, artificially manufacture a reason to leave, for example you've a regular evening class, you're meeting someone, an event you are going to or a particular train you have to catch. Give yourself a reason to get out the door by a particular time and go.

Turn off your tech

Don't keep checking and responding to work emails and messages when you are not at work. If you start responding then it will become expected and other people will feel they need to respond too – and then everyone is working outside of work. If it's a real emergency then they will find a way to get in touch. Mostly it can wait.

Agree priorities

If you are resentfully working long hours just to get through the workload, then go and see your manager at least once a week to agree your priorities and discuss what you feel can reasonably be achieved in the time available. Most people don't mind working extra hours occasionally but continually working long hours just to keep the day to day workload under control is untenable for you – and the organisation.

Assertive but helpful

If your boss is insistent you stay late then offer to look at it very first thing in the morning, guarantee they'll have the work by lunchtime or suggest that you go back and re-negotiate the deadline. Show you won't be coerced and they are likely to back off, it may even enhance your career prospects. Being assertive and dealing positively with a potential conflict situation illustrates your leadership potential far more than someone willing to be a doormat.

Virtual presenteeism

Research shows that those who work virtually, either from home or other locations, often work the longest hours of all – finding it difficult to switch off and over-compensating for their absence from the office by wanting to be super-productive to prove their worth. It's especially important that virtual workers give themselves a 'home time'.

It's good for employers too

Probably everyone is hoping someone will go home first – including your manager. It's okay to have a life. Your employer should want you to have a life – if nothing else because miserable, oppressed people are unlikely to be engaged high performers, let alone good ambassadors for the company so it's in their interests too.

Be clear on your own boundaries

It may be that you're happy to work late at home as long as you can be home for the school run. Negotiate your own 'on' and 'off' times but be clear about keeping them distinct. There is always work you can be doing, but apart from emergency issues most things will wait till the next day.

Think about leaving

There are some professions where, culturally, there is a demanding working hours culture, particularly hospitality, teaching, investment banking, legal firms, etc. As an individual it can be difficult to single-handedly challenge an entrenched system so unless you have a particularly supportive boss, you may need to think about changing sector or job if you want to have a reasonable work/life balance.

EXERCISE 4

RECLAIMING YOUR WORK/ LIFE BALANCE

Let's identify some practical actions you can take which will improve the work/life balance issues you have pinpointed. To help, I have included some suggestions below, but do add as many others as you can that are relevant for you.

At work	Tick if you want to action this
Leave work on time	☐
Reclaim lunch hours and take sensible breaks	☐
Resist checking emails at weekends	☐
Ask to work flexible hours	☐
Avoid rush-hour traffic	☐
Set realistic work deadlines	☐
Delegate where you can	☐
Say no to unreasonable requests	☐
Create 'do not disturb' times at work	☐
Manage demanding people more effectively	☐
Talk to your boss about any work/life issues	☐
Work more efficiently	☐
Write a to-do list with priorities for the day	☐
Set realistic goals for yourself and others	☐
Take all your annual leave!	☐

4 AN OBJECTIVE ASSESSMENT

So far we have looked at your career from a number of different perspectives. We have taken an initial career health check and explored both your inner landscape and your life outside work. The aim has been to give you the opportunity to express your emotions, frustrations, conflicts and concerns in a structured way. They are important, they matter to you and the exercises are a way for you to articulate the career issues that drive or trouble you.

However, as human beings we often tend to focus on all the things that are wrong about a given situation and ignore some of the good things. Looking back on your exercises you may notice this in your answers. Are they more negative than you were expecting?

Don't jump to conclusions

When individuals are in an uncomfortable career situation, their emotions can make their thinking one-sided and make it more difficult for them to see what is in their best interests.

For instance, I speak to many individuals who tell me they want to hand their notice in, even though they haven't another job to go to.

They haven't considered that it can take time to find another role; that unemployment is very stressful; and that it is often easier to find another job while you are still working. It's important to take all this into account when making the decision to resign, and not act purely on emotion.

Equally, I talk to many people who assume, sometimes wrongly, that the only way to progress their career is to leave their current job. They find it easier to move to a new company than have an honest conversation with their manager about their career development.

> *I liked my organisation but just felt like I was treading water so I started applying externally for jobs and got a job offer. When I told my boss I was handing my notice in they said they would be really sorry to lose me and what would make me stay? I said that I had been frustrated that I hadn't been more involved in strategy. The next day they came back and offered me a role as part of the strategy team, which was just fantastic. I wished I had talked to them earlier and saved myself time and anguish.*
>
> **Amelia**

In fact, if you do a good job for your organisation, they are likely to want to keep you and so may be willing to find ways to help you in your career progression. But unless you ask, you will never know. It makes sense to at least make sure you are aware of any internal options before you decide to go.

This final chapter in Part 1 is designed to help you take a more dispassionate view of your current career situation and examine both the positive and the negative aspects equally.

TIP

Listening to your emotions is important because they are telling you an important truth – but it's unlikely to be the whole truth.

EXERCISE 5

VALUES QUESTIONNAIRE

This exercise will help you think about the things that are important to you in your career and help you assess to what extent these are currently being met or where there are gaps.

1. Tick the 10 work values in the list on the following page that are the most important to you.
2. Rank them in importance, with 10 being the most important and 1 the least important. Feel free to add any others you feel are relevant to you.
3. From your top 10 list, mark whether those values are currently being met or not.

TIP

If you are not working at the moment, you may wish to complete this with reference to a previous job or jobs.

Value	Ranking 1–10 (10 = most important)	Currently being met Y/N
Financial reward		
Recognised as high performer		
To be well liked		
Freedom to work how you want		
Change and variety		
Work/life balance		
Work with like-minded people		
Power and influence		
To be a change agent		
Social contact with others		
Using creativity and self-expression		
Expert status		
Personal development and growth		
Make a positive difference to society		
Working to live rather than the other way round		
Earn as much money as possible		
Ascend the corporate career ladder		
Appreciated at work		
Identification with the purpose of the organisation		
Opportunities to travel		
Using physical skills and abilities		
To become well known		
Ethical working in line with your beliefs		
Role that supports your health needs		
Achieve significant things		
Collaborative environment		
Ownership of your work		
Busy or calm environment		

Particular workplace location		
Intellectual challenge		
Sense of belonging		
Caring environment		
Family-friendliness		
Freedom to structure your day		
Strong workplace relationships		
Fun		
Flexible working		
Supportive environment		
Ability to innovate and be a pioneer		
Social status/prestige in role/organisation		
Work with stimulating people		
Security and predictability		
Working outdoors/physically active		
Competitive environment		
To be entrepreneurial		
Variety and change		
Other values:		

4. Which of your key values are being met and which aren't and why?
    Remember to focus on the positives as well as the negatives.

Values being met	Values not being met

EXAMPLE

Values being met	Values not being met
I am paid relatively well for what I do so I am able to enjoy a comfortable lifestyle. I have social status because others see my role as very interesting and want to talk about it. I like this but it isn't really as glamorous as other people think it is. I like the travel aspects of my job.	Not able to use my creativity and self-expression: I've felt very stifled in previous roles. I am a creative person and I think I can bring a fresh approach and new ideas but the organisations I've worked for have been very rigid. Developed ideas but don't feel they were given proper consideration. Stopped even trying. I want to work in an environment where ideas are welcomed. *Malik*

From this exercise you should be able to see that, even if the job you are in currently is not perfect, there are some values that are being met and which are positive.

Let's continue to look at both the good and the bad aspects of your current career situation. The aim is for you to be able to see both sides of the coin. For the following exercise, put on your analytical hat and set your emotions to one side.

EXERCISE 6

CAREER POSITIVES AND NEGATIVES

1. Write down as many positive things as you can about your current career situation, for example the fact that it's close to home or you like the product line you are working with.

2. Write down as many negative things as you can about your current career situation, for example any values that aren't being met, a threat of redundancy or lack of opportunities.

3. Make the lists as balanced as you can – have an equal number of items on each side.

TIP

You might find it helpful to ask someone else to play devil's advocate with you if one side is more heavily weighted than the other.

Positives	Negatives

EXAMPLE

Positives	Negatives
Good access to training.	Threat of redundancy.
Might be opportunities with the new restructuring.	Staff cuts will mean more work.
Some flexibility about working hours.	Don't know how service will continue with less staff.
Like working in this industry.	Will have to compete with colleagues.
Pension benefits.	Pay freeze.
	Gillian

Did you find it easy to fill in both the positive and the negative columns? Or was it far easier to do one side than the other?

When people feel strongly about something – and they usually do when they are dissatisfied with elements in their career – they will be biased and then will look for evidence to support that view. Make sure you have acted on point 3 of the exercise, and have tried to make your list as balanced as possible.

The useful thing about this exercise is that it forces you to consider both perspectives and challenge your own assumptions. You may still make the same decisions you would have done before thinking about it, but at least you have fully considered the counter-argument.

> *I am very comfortable in my current job. It's close to home, relatively secure and although the pay isn't great, it's steady. However, looking at the negatives, it made me realise that I am in danger of becoming de-skilled as I am not doing half of the things I am capable of or learning anything new. I think that could make me very vulnerable if I had to find another job.*
>
> **Rashid**

Identifying positive changes to make

Now that we have completed a full career diagnostic of your current situation, let's focus on the positive changes you want to bring about in your career.

EXERCISE 7

I WANT …

1. Review all the exercises in Part 1 of this book to gather your thoughts and then complete the following 'I want …' sentences.

2. You may want to include:
    *   things you want to be different, e.g. 'I want to be paid more'
    *   things you want to be the same, e.g. 'I want to carry on working part time'
    *   emotional wants and needs, e.g. 'I want to rediscover my motivation'
    *   areas of uncertainty that you want to resolve, e.g. 'I want to understand my career options.'

Don't censor or edit this list. Write down everything that is important to you.

TIP

You are encouraged to be demanding in this exercise. Write down everything that is important to you for the future – both practically and emotionally. Include them all.

I want ...

I want ...

I want ...

I want ...

I want ...

I want ...

I want ...

I want ...

EXAMPLE

I want ... *to feel that I have made a difference to the world.*

I want ... *to make good use of my time.*

I want ... *to work with people who are passionate about the cause.*

I want ... *to work with an organisation that has power.*

I want ... *to safeguard my earnings.*

I want ... *to know whether I should stay or find a new job.*

Michael

In the above exercise you have identified your career needs and wants for the future. Bear these in mind as you work through the rest of this book. They will be important touchstones when we come to look at your options for the future in Part 5.

The reality of your situation

As we have seen throughout Part 1, your career situation is unique, complex and multi-faceted. Whatever your circumstances, you should now have a deeper insight into and some fresh perspectives on your current career situation.

In the reflections exercise below, capture your thoughts from working through the book so far. This will a handy reference point for later.

EXERCISE 8

REFLECTING ON PART 1

Review the following exercises in this section:

- Exercise 1: Career Health Check (page 2)
- Exercise 2: Picture of your world (page 7)
- Exercise 3: Work/life balance assessment (page 17)
- Exercise 4: Reclaiming your work/life balance (page 21)
- Exercise 5: Values questionnaire (page 25)
- Exercise 6: Career positives and negatives (page 28)
- Exercise 7: I want ... (page 30)

1. What have you found particularly helpful in these exercises?
2. Are there any themes, words or phrases that seem very appropriate or keep popping up?
3. What emotions have you felt and why do you think you responded in that way?
4. Are there any actions you can take that will make a difference?

TIP

Be alert to any recurring emotive words or phrases that you use as this is likely to be very expressive of your situation and thinking.

My reflections on where I am now

Action points

EXAMPLE

The exercises in this section really hit home for me that I'm spending all my time working and not enough time having fun. I need to work harder at my social life. I get so focused on my career to the exclusion of everything else – and it's not good for me. The relationship part has definitely suffered and I need to invest some time in this.

Because I've had to take over the role of a colleague who has been made redundant, I'm feeling quite stressed because of the increased workload. Have been getting migraines – and been grumpy with my partner because it's really been getting to me. I don't want to fail – because I don't want to be made redundant, but the more stressed I get, the less capable I feel.

I probably need to discuss with my manager what her priorities are rather than trying to do everything at once, which is unachievable. She has just kind of left me to it, but I think I need to understand her priorities and then I can choose where to direct my energies rather than trying to do everything all at the same time. If that doesn't help, I think I need to look for another job.

I think my migraines will probably reduce if I'm less stressed and also remember to eat regularly rather than skipping meals because I'm too busy. I know family life will improve if I'm less stressed.

Action points

1. *Make an appointment to discuss priorities with my manager.*

2. *Start job-searching.*

3. *Take lunch breaks and eat properly.*

Liz

We will revisit this reflections exercise again when we look back on your career coaching journey in Part 9.

In Part 1, we have looked in detail at your current situation from both a career and a personal perspective and identified your priorities for change.

However, you haven't just magically arrived at this point in time. You have a long and interesting history that has brought you here, comprising important events, key decisions and formative experiences. Let's look at your journey!

How you got here

Understanding your past enables you to put your current situation in context. This will include formative events and other influences that helped you become the person you are.

We'll look at the successes you've experienced and the obstacles you've faced and what you have learned about yourself in good times and bad.

If we can determine the behaviours and strategies that have worked for you in the past, as well as those that perhaps didn't, then we can anticipate potential difficulties and make sure you are well equipped with the resources you will need to overcome them.

So in Part 2, we are going to look backwards to help us go forwards.

In this section we will:

■ look at your key life events

■ create an autobiography

■ discover the key influences that have shaped your personal history

■ document your work history in detail

5 YOUR PERSONAL HISTORY

In your past there will have been a number of turning points where you made career decisions. Some of those decisions may have been well thought out, while others may have been more spontaneous or even forced upon you.

How far has your career to date been planned? Have there been times when your career has been going well and other times when it hit the doldrums or had to swerve because of an unforeseen event?

> I had to look after my mum from an early age as she was very ill. Becoming a nurse was a natural extension of looking after my mum.
>
> **Mary**

Alongside your career, you are likely to have also had peaks and troughs in your life. Most people will have faced, at some time or other, difficult circumstances such as unemployment, ill health, relationship breakdowns, financial difficulties or the loss of a loved one. These can be extremely stressful and their effects can be felt for a long time afterwards. Have any of these difficulties influenced your career journey to date and if so, what impact did they have or, indeed, continue to have?

> Work was so stressful that I became really ill; so I quit my job, went travelling and came back in a much better state of mind. Found myself a more junior job with less pressure. I'm so much happier.
>
> **Ed**

We are going to look at how you have dealt with these different scenarios in your life and career.

Try to approach the following exercises as though you are a historian sifting through the evidence or an author commissioned to profile an important figure. Be your own biographer – warts and all! Let's hear your story.

You may find that some of these exercises arouse some surprisingly powerful emotions, especially if they touch on particularly sensitive areas. If this happens you might either find it wonderfully cathartic or perhaps unsettling so be aware of your own limits and go only as deeply as you feel comfortable.

TIP

These exercises are very personal, so stay within your comfort zone when contemplating any deeply sensitive areas.

Let's start by looking at the most significant events that have happened to you in your life to date.

EXERCISE 9

MY LIFE EVENTS

1. On the diagram on the following page or on a separate sheet of paper, plot the key moments and events in your life to date, starting from birth on the left side of the line until the current date. Examples could include:
   - early life experiences
   - educational history and achievements
   - your work experiences
   - happy events, for example falling in love or winning a competition
   - traumatic events, for example accidents, illness or a bereavement
   - achievements, for example awards, successful projects or community impact
   - challenges, for example redundancy, relationship breakdown or money problems
   - health issues for you or others
   - other significant events, for example travel adventures, building your own house, starting a business or meeting a mentor

Positive times

Age 0 7 14 21 28 35 42 49

Negative times

2. For each event, on the chart mark what happened when, and how positive or negative an experience it was (refer to the example on page 40 to help you).

3. Now answer these questions to help you debrief this exercise.

What did it feel like doing this exercise?

Which were the happiest times in your life, and why?

When there were difficult times, what helped you get through?

When were you most successful at dealing with change, and why?

Write down three key points that emerge for you from this exercise:

1.

2.

3.

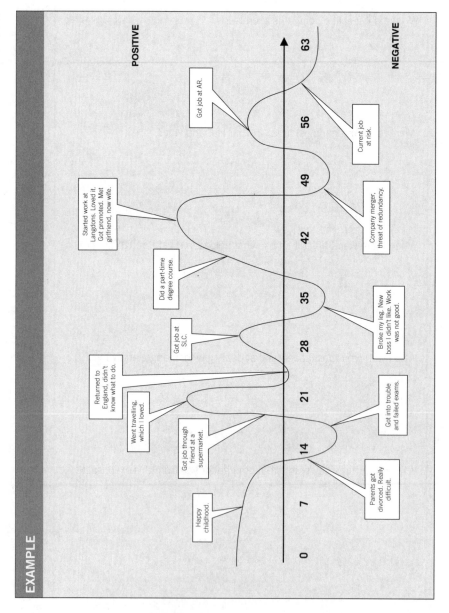

POSITIVE

NEGATIVE

0   7   14   21   28   35   42   49   56   63

Happy childhood.

Parents got divorced. Really difficult.

Got job through friend at a supermarket.

Went travelling, which I loved.

Returned to England, didn't know what to do.

Got into trouble and failed exams.

Got job at SLC.

Broke my leg. New boss I didn't like. Work was not good.

Did a part-time degree course.

Started work at Langdons. Loved it. Got promoted. Met girlfriend, now wife.

Company merger, threat of redundancy.

Got job at AR.

Current job at risk.

EXAMPLE

What did it feel like doing this exercise?

Okay. But surprised how much it still rankles that I didn't do as well as I should have in my school exams.

Which were the happiest times in your life, and why?

Loved my role at Langdons. Think this was because there was a real team spirit and it felt like we were doing stuff that mattered. Met my wife around same time. Both work and personal life were great.

When there were difficult times, what helped you get through?

It was horrible when I came back to England and I kept getting rejected for jobs I knew I could do. But I just had to get on with it so kept applying and eventually heard about the job at SLC from a friend.

When I broke my leg I had a new boss whose first experience of me was being off on sick leave. The relationship was never a good one. Decided to study for a degree as wanted to prove to the boss that I was capable. Knew I had to take my career development in my own hands because my boss would not help me. Felt great handing in my notice when I got my new job.

When were you most successful at dealing with change, and why?

It was difficult when Langdons got taken over as they wanted to do things differently. I did tell them when I thought they were making mistakes but also said when I thought their ideas were better. Think they respected my openness and that I wasn't just being awkward for the sake of it. I also helped persuade others to accept difficult change and I think that this bought me a lot of credibility with the new manager. As a result I still had a job while many of my colleagues left or were made redundant. Wife was very supportive throughout.

Write down three key points that emerge for you from this exercise.

1. *I'm probably more resilient than I thought, have been through some difficult times but have been quite determined to get what I want.*

2. *Bit of a hang-up about my school education – feel like I'm not as good academically as others. However, getting my degree helped.*

3. *Relationships at work have been as important as the job itself – particularly my relationship with my manager. My wife is a great sounding board.*

James

This exercise charts the key points in your career and life history. While it is interesting to look back on significant events, it is the way you have *responded* to these circumstances that is of particular interest in terms of your career coaching.

Do you think that other people might have responded to those events in a similar way? How would people who were close to you at the time have described the way you dealt with them?

> *It was really hard when my marriage broke up. I was very low. Work proved a useful distraction, kept me busy and helped preserve the little of what was left of my self-esteem.*
>
> **Steve**

EXERCISE 10

YOUR AUTOBIOGRAPHY

This autobiographical exercise takes us beyond life events to look at some of the other formative influences and experiences that have helped shape your story and your career to date.

1. Write your autobiography, focusing in particular on stories and experiences that you consider helped shape the person you are today. You may find this easier to write on a separate piece of paper or as a downloadable document on your computer.

2. Write it with yourself in mind as the intended audience. It's up to you whether you want to show it to anyone else.

3. Feel free to write as much as you wish. You can write it in a very structured chronological way or be more free-flowing. You might find it easier to break down your autobiography into seven-year chunks, for example ages 0–7, 7–14, 14–21 and so on, as we did in Exercise 9.

4. You might include:

   - earliest memories
   - family experiences
   - educational experiences at school
   - early career decisions – how they were made
   - key relationships
   - things you made happen
   - regrets
   - major turning points in your life
   - highlights and proudest moments
   - your toughest challenges and how you dealt with them.

TIP

In your writing, express your thoughts and opinions on your story, as well as the facts.

My autobiography

EXAMPLE

Age 0–7

Earliest I can remember is sitting on the lawn at our old house looking at the sky. From an early age really loved football, would kick one around for hours. Always had a lot of energy and mum used to describe me as a tornado – always rushing around at full speed.

Age 7–14

Remember doing quite well at primary school. I remember coming top of the class in the maths test and people being pleased with me. I think mum and dad were hoping I might get into the local grammar school but when I failed the test they were really supportive and told me that it didn't matter. I was a bit disappointed, but not overly because lots of my friends were going to the local comprehensive which made up for it. However, at secondary school more interested in football than anything else so I didn't pay much attention in class.

Age 14–21

Got in with the anti-school crowd. Mum and dad got divorced when I was 15 but I was mainly just ignoring them anyway, making sure that I was out of the house and not in the middle of one of their arguments. I suddenly became the 'man of the house' – bit resentful but in some ways it did make me grow up. Became really important to bring money into the house so when I left school at 16 took the first job I could get that would pay money right away. Couldn't go into higher education even if I'd wanted to.

First few years at work was just working to get the money in – to bring money home and pay for my social life. Didn't think about having a career.

Age 21–28

Found a new job at Peterson's and had a really good manager who I think spotted something in me. Really encouraged me – and I started to feel that maybe I did have career prospects. Got promoted and this did wonders for my confidence. However, aware of a bit of a glass ceiling for those who didn't start on the graduate programme with the company and knew I could only progress so far. Stayed two years but then decided to join Smith's where I could get rewarded on results rather than qualifications. Especially important as was getting married and the money to build a life together was important.

> Age 28–35
>
> *Had been doing really well in sales and getting increasingly interested in marketing. But same old problem of qualifications came up – I was never going to get the opportunity to get my manager's job without a sales and marketing qualification. Very reluctant to do it. What if I failed it? Where would that leave me? Actually decided to leave and work for smaller company where qualifications not so important.*
>
> *Regret this I think. If I'd done the qualification earlier it would have been tough, but in the long run would probably have been worth it.*
>
> Age 35–42
>
> *Have two kids and wife not working. Still considering whether or not I should study for a qualification. Hugely expensive and not sure whether I have the time to commit to it. Feel I haven't progressed as far as I should because of my lack of qualifications. Have steered clear of bigger companies because I don't think I stand a chance of being hired, even though I think I could do a much better job than the managers who are there already.*
>
> **Ralph**

You may have found exercises 9 and 10 cathartic; a way of looking back on your career so far – the highs and the lows. You will have been able to see from your autobiography the range of different influences, as well as events that have shaped your history to date.

We are going to examine those influences in more detail in the next chapter. These influences will have had great power in the past and many will continue to do so in the future. They are probably shaping your career right now, without you even being aware of it.

6 KEY CAREER INFLUENCES

In your autobiography in Exercise 10, you traced your personal and career history from your early years to the present day to provide perspective on how your personal story has evolved.

This chapter is going to look more closely at some of the key influences that have been instrumental in helping shape your story. It will include elements such as the significant people in your life, aspects of your social identity and other formative influences. Read through this chapter and then in Exercise 11 on page 53 we'll capture your thoughts.

Significant people

Your family

When you were growing up, your family will have helped shape your sense of identity and interpreted the external world for you. Our parents will have drawn our earliest boundaries, instilled the 'dos' and 'don'ts' and we would have started to define our sense of who we are and how the world operates in response to this. Those early ground rules are likely to be embedded somewhere in our consciousness whether we fully accepted them or even rebelled against them.

> *My mum and dad were very modest really – not what you call high-flyers. But when I was the first one in my family to go to university, they were so proud. It made me feel exceptional. My upbringing I think has given me great personal self-confidence – that I can do well because of me and my efforts, not because of privilege.*
>
> **Ian**

Family is often very influential when it comes to making early career choices. At an early age, with little or no career experience, it's a huge decision and young people will naturally look to adults they trust for guidance and validation.

The expectations of the family can be very powerful. There may have been pressure for you to do well at school, to pursue a particular kind of career path or even to follow in the family business. They may have had different expectations of you than your siblings. Alternatively they may have had a 'hands-free' or even uninterested approach that you may have found either liberating or unsupportive.

> *Both my parents were teachers, so it just seemed to be a natural choice.*
>
> **Sophie**

If you are working in a similar field to any members of your family, have you wondered whether this is because you have a shared aptitude for a particular type of job or because you are more aware of this career path as a realistic possibility. You can often see professional threads in generations of families pursuing similar paths as teachers, journalists, the military, artists, banking, healthcare, entrepreneurs, etc.

What influence do you feel your family had on your career expectations?

Partner

Romantic relationships, current and past, may also have influenced your career. You may have made career choices that enabled you to be closer to your partner or even decided to set up business together. Your partner may have been supportive in respect of your career, competitive or perhaps dismissive, or over-reliant on you being the breadwinner. Raising children may also have required a re-balancing of your career priorities within the household.

> *I have to travel a lot for work and I know that my partner finds this really difficult as she has a high-flying career but when I am away she needs to look after the kids. However, if I want to get ahead, I'm going to need to do more travelling, not less. Which do I put first – family or career?*
>
> **Sam**

> *I know that if it wasn't for my husband I would never have dreamed of setting up my own business. He has been incredibly supportive and has helped me with the things I dreaded, for example VAT. Without him it wouldn't have been possible.*
>
> **Shirley**

Have your romantic relationships had any effect on your career?

Role models

In our careers, we come across both good and bad role models: managers who were the embodiment of good leadership; and those who were pretty dreadful. We're likely to have picked up some good and bad habits from both.

> *My first boss was always ruthlessly honest; this made you work really hard to get his approval. I don't think I've ever worked so hard for anyone. I've always tried to use that same approach. People don't always like it, but I think they respect it*
>
> **Utsav**

> *I have a colleague who has a great ability to calm down any fraught situation. She stays calm herself, uses humour, and really listens to the other person. Whenever I'm in a similar situation, I use some of the same tactics which I learned from observing her.*
>
> **Jane**

Who have your role models been? Perhaps there is a friend, ex-manager, business colleague, a community figure or someone famous who has inspired you. What is it about their example that you feel is important to you?

Educational experiences

Your experiences at school and in higher education are likely to feature some of your earliest brushes with success and failure. Academic achievements may determine whether some professional routes are open to you in the early stages of your career but it can also have a lasting effect on your professional confidence.

> *I was so proud to get my degree; for me, it showed the world that I could do it – that I had potential and I was as good as anyone else.*
>
> **Charlotte**

While those with good academic qualifications may be proud or take for granted their achievements, people sometimes have more complex feelings about academic disappointments, whether it is failed school exams or discontentment with a 2:1 when they were aiming for a 1st in their degree.

Some will use it as an additional motivator and be very driven to succeed to prove to the world their capabilities. They might even wear their lack of

Do you feel that there have been different expectations because you are male or female? If so, how has that played out in the workplace or when applying for jobs?

Social identity

What different communities or groups do you feel you identify with? This might be in line with your spiritual or political beliefs, your class, cultural or ethnic background or your affiliation with particular places or groups. This could include the places where you or your parents were born or where you now live.

> *In my community the ultimate ambition is to be a doctor or lawyer. If you are not, there is a sense of disappointment that you didn't work hard enough …*
>
> **Nita**

Have those communities ever shaped your thinking about your career? Were there particular types of roles or organisations that were held in higher regard or were more familiar to you and therefore may have influenced your choices?

And in terms of your social identity has this ever been an advantage or disadvantage to you at work? For instance, while we know there is legislation to prevent discrimination on the grounds of race, gender, sexual orientation and disabilities, marital and civil partnership status, pregnancy, age, religion and beliefs, we also know that conscious and unconscious bias exists in the workplace and that can be problematic.

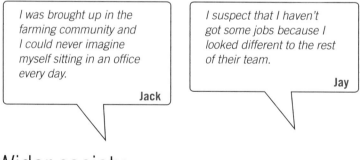

> *I was brought up in the farming community and I could never imagine myself sitting in an office every day.*
>
> **Jack**

> *I suspect that I haven't got some jobs because I looked different to the rest of their team.*
>
> **Jay**

Wider society

You and your career don't exist in a vacuum and there will have been all kinds of societal factors that will have directly or indirectly influenced your career to date. This includes changing values in society, new technologies, market booms and busts, as well as globalisation and new ways of working.

Perhaps there were times when you've changed career not because you wanted to but because demand had diminished or because wider political pressures had made your job untenable. Maybe a growing acceptance of flexible working made it possible for you to return from maternity leave which would otherwise have been difficult.

Where might wider society have had an impact on your career to date?

Having reflected on some of these different influences, now complete Exercise 11 and make some notes on your thoughts.

> *Although I loved my job I knew I had to get out of teaching because the political meddling was having such a demoralising effect on me.*
>
> **Kerry**

EXERCISE 11

YOUR CAREER INFLUENCES

Practical influences	People influences	Wider influences
Financial	Parents	Community
Security	Family	Religious
Location	Peers/colleagues	Political
Job availability	Friends	Societal
Qualifications	Teachers	Media
Career experiences	Role models	Gender
Disability	Partner	Social class
Training	Managers	Discrimination

1. From the lists above, write down below which factors you believe have had an influence on your career to date and why. These might be very practical things such as the availability of jobs in your local area or funding to go to university. A disability or financial needs may have meant that some jobs were more feasible for you than others or there may have been significant people who made an impression on your thinking about your career. Add on any other influential factors you feel are important.

2. How do you think those influences affected you in comparison with those in a similar position, such as your siblings or peers?

3. Which of these influences do you believe will continue to be influential for you in the future?

4. There is an example of this exercise on page 55.

My influences

EXAMPLE

MY INFLUENCES

Family – *they discouraged me from pursuing art, which I really wanted to do, as they didn't see it as a proper job.*

Gender – *as a man I think there is an expectation that I will always be the breadwinner and that this is my responsibility above everything else.*

Social class – *my father didn't think that an 'artistic' job was a proper job for a man.*

Art teacher – *was wonderful, very supportive; only increased my frustration with my parents.*

Location – *took first job that would take me away from home so that I could live my own life.*

Career experiences – *found that marketing at least had some creativity to it.*

Partner – *she relies on me to be the breadwinner but sometimes I think why can't she go out to work and I will stay at home, look after the kids and paint.*

Role model – *my kids. I love the way they play with paint, they are so free and spontaneous.*

Peers – *I'm not that interested in my peers at work. Benchmark myself against fellow artists.*

My brother and sister have all followed very conventional careers and been very successful. Have always really struggled to throw off that sense of frustration – that I haven't been able to follow my heart and do a job that I've loved. Work has always been solely about bringing the money in – nothing else; and this is largely how I continue to think about work.

I wonder, though, whether there is some other role that I can do, which would interest me more than my current job but which was realistic salary-wise?

Ray

This chapter has shown that your choices in your career are likely to have been heavily influenced by a range of personal and societal factors. Some of these will still be very relevant, while others may have diminished in importance over time.

Are you surprised by your answers to Exercise 11? Perhaps you didn't realise your family had such a strong influence on your past career choices, or how a particular role model had inspired you. Whatever you have been struck by, keep this in mind as you work through the rest of Part 2.

7 YOUR CAREER HISTORY

Employers pay very close attention to your job history because they want to understand not only whether you have the skills and experience to fill their vacancy, but also the rationale for your career decisions, your career progression and your relationships with previous employers.

In this chapter we are going to put a magnifying glass up to each job you've worked in and examine it closely. You need to understand your job history if you are to explain it to anyone else. Analysing your job experiences will also reveal any common themes about your likes, dislikes and any recurrent challenges.

Don't worry if your career to date has not followed what you think is a standard pattern. Many people change their career focus, not just while they are experimenting in the early stages of their career, but later on too.

In addition, most people will have had career breaks, career mistakes, periods of unemployment, and temporary or voluntary jobs along the way. These are standard features of most modern careers rather than the exception.

Whatever your career experiences have been, all of them will have provided intense learning experiences, testing your capabilities, extending your knowledge and leading you to other career possibilities.

So let's look chronologically at your different work experiences and what they tell us about you.

We will revisit Exercise 12 when we create your Career Summary document in Part 9.

EXAMPLE

How have you typically found a new job?

I found most of my roles through hearing about them from someone I know.

What were the differences between the jobs you enjoyed and those you didn't?

Career highlights were working in the TV production company. Loved it. Exciting. Fast-moving. Got to meet lots of interesting people. Very lively. Also working on the conferences for Jays. Liked being front of house – doing the PR.

Got very miserable in a couple of jobs and stayed there far longer than I should. Only moved in the end because the threat of redundancy eventually spurred me on. Not very proactive.

The jobs I enjoyed all involved working with people who were great fun. They made me laugh. Lots of energy. Used to socialise after work.

Great team spirit. Worked hard. Played hard.

Jobs where I was unhappy were ones where I felt that my personality just didn't suit the company. Felt like a fish out of water. Didn't have my sense of humour. Just didn't seem to connect. They were far too straight for me.

Were there any difficulties that surfaced in more than one job, for example bullying or a difficult workplace relationship?

Some organisations just didn't feel like I fitted in – they were much too corporate for me. I like a more relaxed atmosphere.

Mel

Career luck or career design?

I hope that what you have started to see emerging in this section is a sense of how your career and the person you are today have been shaped by how you have responded to a wide range of influences, events and circumstances.

Even if you feel that your career to date has happened more by accident than design, you will have chosen to accept certain opportunities and

> *In my last job everyone was constantly whinging and moaning about the organisation. It was relentless and very depressing. I didn't want to work in such a negative environment so I worked hard to get myself out as quickly as I could. Why are the others still there if they are so unhappy?*
>
> **Pam**

not others. You may have put yourself forward for some roles or hidden yourself from view. You will have decided to tackle some career problems while maybe deciding to do nothing about others.

You are not where you are solely by chance!

Professor Richard Wiseman's book *The Luck Factor* (Arrow, 2004) was written following his research into why some individuals seem to have better luck than others. He examined the beliefs and experiences of lucky and unlucky people. From his research he distilled four simple techniques commonly used by lucky people. You may not win the lottery with his techniques, but his research showed that these behaviours can undoubtedly influence the odds as to whether good things are more likely to happen to you.

Maximise chance opportunities

Lucky people are skilled at creating, noticing and acting upon chance opportunities. They do this in various ways, including networking, adopting a relaxed attitude to life and by being open to new experiences.

Listen to lucky hunches

Lucky people make effective decisions by listening to their intuition and gut feelings. In addition, they take steps to actively boost their intuitive abilities by, for example, meditating and clearing their mind of other thoughts.

Expect good fortune

Lucky people are certain that the future is going to be full of good fortune. These expectations become self-fulfilling prophecies by helping lucky people persist in the face of failure and shape their interactions with others in a positive way.

Turn bad luck to good

Lucky people employ various psychological techniques to cope with, and often even thrive upon, the ill fortune that comes their way. For example, they spontaneously imagine how things could have been worse, do not dwell on their ill fortune, and take control of the situation.

Professor Richard Wiseman, **The Luck Factor**

Now think about all the times in your career when you felt that you had a lucky break. You may have had a chance meeting with someone who later hired you or your application landed on the manager's desk just when they were looking for someone like you.

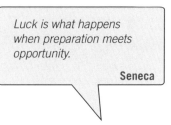

Luck is what happens when preparation meets opportunity.

Seneca

Was it just luck? The opportunity may have landed at your feet, but you needed to capitalise on it. You would still have had to impress the employer that you could do the job. You would have needed to take the initiative to make the application or decide to talk to the stranger in the room at that networking event who turned out to be such a useful contact for you. The risky job move that worked out brilliantly you could have rejected because you wanted to play safe. If you hadn't decided to push for management training with your employer, then perhaps you would never have been ready to step into your boss's shoes when they left unexpectedly.

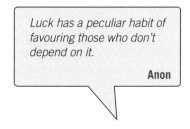

Luck has a peculiar habit of favouring those who don't depend on it.

Anon

In your career, you make your own luck!

Looking at your history

This section has been a fairly intense and detailed look at your personal and career history. We have looked at the key events, your life story, major influences and your career experiences.

EXERCISE 13

REFLECTING ON PART 2

Review the following exercises:

- Exercise 9: My life events (page 37)
- Exercise 10: Your autobiography (page 42)
- Exercise 11: Your career influences (page 53)
- Exercise 12: Your work history (page 58)

Note down any other thoughts or observations that are prompted when you read your own words. These might include:

1.   What you have learned about yourself from these exercises.

2.   What positive things about you have emerged.

3.   What advice you might have given to your past self.

4.   Are there things you would do differently in the future?

5.   What actions can you take in the future that will build on your learning from the past?

- -

Write down your thoughts below.

My reflections on my history

Action points

EXAMPLE

I'm thankful to my parents for pushing me hard. Even now I hate to do anything that might disappoint my parents. Friends are definitely a big influence; I am competitive so I do want to do better than them career-wise. I don't want to get left behind. Salary is a benchmark for me in this. If I can keep up with or exceed the salary of my friends then I feel I am doing well. I can see that I am quite an impatient person. On the one hand, this is good because it has meant that if something isn't right then I've quickly done something about it. But on occasion I think that I jumped too fast. I knew that I didn't want what I had, so I looked for the fastest way out, rather than thinking about what was the right next move for me. I have been like this in my jobs but also my relationships too. Maybe I need to slow down a bit. Think before I jump.

Action points

1. *Slow down my decision-making.*

2. *Do my research more thoroughly on any new job before I accept it.*

3. *Research typical salary levels for those in my field to draw comparisons.*

Alex

We will revisit this reflections exercise when we look back on your career coaching journey in Part 9.

PART 3

What you can offer: your career capital

Let me introduce you to a concept called 'career capital'. Put simply, career capital is the skills, knowledge and attributes that you have to offer a potential employer. The value of your career capital will depend on its relevance to a particular job, employer demand and expectations, and how you compare with other candidates in the job market.

Whenever you apply for a job you will need to prove your career capital to the employer and this section will provide the information you need to help you do this in preparation for the job market.

In this section we will:

- gather the evidence to identify the skills and expertise you possess

- prove the contribution you can make to an organisation

- uncover other elements that enhance your career capital

8 IDENTIFYING YOUR SKILLS

Whatever career path you take, your skills will be the currency you take on your journey. This chapter will help you assess which of your skills are of high value and any that you undervalue. We'll also identify the skills you may want to develop or acquire to improve your future career prospects.

Competencies

You may hear employers refer to skills as 'competencies'. Employers often prefer this term because instead of describing a generic skill, a competence is very practical, showing how that skill has been applied in real-life scenarios. It's the difference, for instance, between saying that a medical receptionist is 'good with people' (skill) or 'experienced in dealing with visitors to the surgery who can be very anxious' (competency-based statement).

Whenever employers are looking to recruit new staff they will specify the particular skills or competences they are looking for. They will usually describe these in job advertisements and the person specification forms that are often attached to job descriptions. When they are considering your CV and questioning you at interview, they will be looking for practical examples of how you have demonstrated the skills they are looking for in your past roles.

Transferable skills

Transferable skills are those which you have been using in one job but which can easily be applied to another. For instance, if you have very strong organisational skills, you might also consider roles that involve co-ordinating people, resources and tasks such as administration, event management or team leadership.

If you are considering a change in role or sector, then your transferable skills can be a useful bridge into your new career situation.

> I worked for 20 years for the council in planning permission and panicked that I would never find another job when I was made redundant. However, when we started to look at my transferable skills, I could see that I am very experienced at dealing with all the complex paperwork and procedures around property issues and good at explaining it to homeowners. I am now working at my local estate agent, which I am really enjoying, where my skills are very relevant.
>
> **Claire**

SKILLS ASSESSMENT

This exercise will help you identify your strongest skills and those you are interested in using in the future. Sometimes you may be very good at something; you just don't want to do it any more.

1. Using a coloured pen, highlight which, in your opinion, are your 5–10 top skills. These should be skills you feel are your strongest skills rather than those you loosely possess.

2. The skills list isn't exhaustive, but it is designed as a useful prompt. Feel free to add any other skills you have that are not on the list.

Adapting	Assembling	Certifying
Administering	Assessing	Chairing
Advising	Auditing	Classifying
Analysing	Briefing	Coaching
Anticipating	Budgeting	Collaborating
Appraising	Building	Collating
Articulating	Calculating	Communication (email)

Communicating (face to face)	Empathising	Investigating
Communicating (telephone)	Empowering	Judging
Computing	Enforcing	Launching
Conceptualising	Estimating	Leading
Constructing	Evaluating	Learning quickly
Consulting	Examining	Lecturing
Controlling	Experimenting	Liaising
Coordinating	Explaining	Lifting
Coping	Facilitating	Listening
Counselling	Filing	Making presentations
Creating	Finalising	Managing
Cultivating	Financing	Managing people
Customer service	Fixing	Marketing
Decision-making	Forecasting	Measuring
Delegating	Generating ideas	Mediating
Demonstrating	Growing plants	Memorising
Designing	Guiding	Mentoring
Detailing	Handling conflict	Modelling
Detecting	Helping	Moderating
Developing	Illustrating	Motivating
Diagnosing	Implementing	Negotiating
Diplomacy	Improving	Networking
Directing	Improvising	Operating
Displaying	Influencing	Ordering
Disproving	Informing	Organising
Dissecting	Initiating	Painting
Disseminating	Innovating	Persuading
Documenting	Inspecting	Piloting
Drafting	Inspiring	Pioneering
Drawing	Installing	Planning
Driving	Interpreting	Precision
Editing	Interviewing	Presenting
Educating	Inventing	Prioritising

Problem-solving	Repairing	Systematising
Procuring	Report writing	Teaching
Proofreading	Representing	Team building
Promoting	Researching	Testing
Public speaking	Restoring	Time management
Publicising	Risk assessment	Training
Purchasing	Scheduling	Trouble-shooting
Quantifying	Selling	Using tools
Raising animals	Setting objectives	Versatility
Reconciling	Simplifying	Visualising
Recording	Sorting	Winning
Recruiting	Structuring	Working to deadlines
Rehabilitating	Summarising	Working under pressure
Relationship building	Supervising	Writing

3. For the skills you have identified as your best skills, think of examples when you have demonstrated your skills in action. These may be skills you use every day or occasionally.

Your key skills	Examples of when you have used these skills
1	
2	

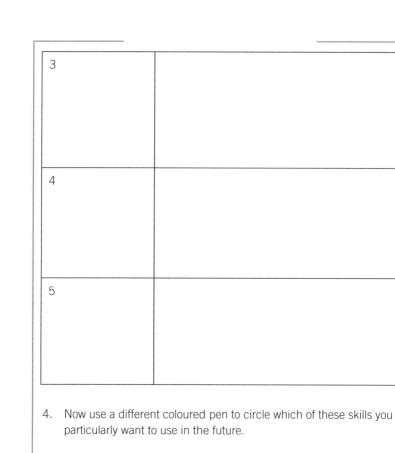

3	
4	
5	

4.   Now use a different coloured pen to circle which of these skills you particularly want to use in the future.

5.   Are there any skills you want to develop further? Perhaps these will help you to do your current job better, improve your promotion prospects or are skills that simply interest you.

Skills I want to use and those I want to develop further

Achievement 1

Achievement 2

Achievement 3

EXAMPLE

I was asked to be the acting manager when my boss went on sick leave. We didn't know how long she was going to be away. I was very new in post but felt very nervous. However, I got stuck in. It was a bit of a baptism by fire because there were lots of things I just didn't know, but I was honest and I became very resourceful at finding out the answers. The other staff were very helpful and supportive – it would have been a nightmare if they hadn't been – but I think they could see I was doing my best and wanted to help me. I did this role for six months and it was fantastic personal development. I know that I also held the department together at what could have been a very tricky time. They gave me an extra payment to reflect my input. I felt pleased that I was able to do a decent job when I was, to be frank, completely out of my depth, and it gave me real confidence that I would be able to manage at that more senior level. The organisation benefited in that they clearly saved money by not having to recruit someone temporarily into the role. They could also see that I was an additional resource they could use over and above the role I was appointed to – and so I was assigned to sit on the Working Group project team.

Kwame

EXERCISE 15 (CONT.)

3. Once you have explored the detail of your key achievements, consider the following and write your thoughts below.

Are there any common elements in the different achievements you have chosen?

What do they say about you to a potential employer?

EXAMPLE

Are there any common elements in the different achievements you have chosen?

All of my achievements show an ability to bring order and structure to an uncertain situation. I'm good at dealing with ambiguity and seeing where we need to go and providing a path to lead us there. I like getting things organised. Working on projects is great.

What do they say about you to a potential employer?

I have excellent organisational skills. You can give me a mess and I will sort it out. Give me your problems and I will enjoy the challenge.

Lee

Demonstrating your worth

Your achievements are just a few examples of the positive contribution you have made to the organisations you have worked with.

There are likely to be many others where you have demonstrated your worth to your employers. They may be less personally satisfying than those in your achievements exercise above, and may be part of your everyday responsibilities, but they are equally of interest. On the following page are some examples.

- Updating a website which increased customer hits by 10%.
- Changing the method of data input to increase database accuracy.
- Revamping a shop window so that it attracted more customers.
- Reducing staff turnover by 5% by introducing a new absence policy.
- Developing new services that generated £20,000 of business in the first month.
- Managing a complex new building project with zero accidents.
- Reorganising a database system to reflect changing management needs.
- Developing a high-performance team with previously under-performing staff.

No matter what job you have worked in, there will always be things you have done that have left the job/team/organisation in a better place than when you arrived. This is very important information for your career capital, regardless of whether you are looking to work in a commercial organisation, a charity or the public sector.

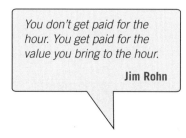

> *You don't get paid for the hour. You get paid for the value you bring to the hour.*
>
> **Jim Rohn**

However, when you are so close to your role and perhaps unused to working in a commercial environment, it can sometimes be tricky to see the wider impact that you have. In this case, you might find it helpful to imagine a scenario where no one was doing your role, or they were doing it extremely badly. What might go wrong? What would the risks to the organisation be? What would the negative consequences be? By doing this you will see that you have been doing a whole host of things that have had a positive impact.

Where you can, try to research whether your department or organisation has any facts and figures that can substantiate the value of the improvements you have made. Look at your departmental targets, management reports, sales figures and your performance evaluations for relevant information.

> *As an administrator I struggled to see how I had 'added value' to the organisation. However, when I started to think about it, there were lots of things that I had done that were important. If I didn't get the invoices out on time, the company's cash flow could have been jeopardised. If I didn't take customer contact details accurately, a potential sale could have been lost.*
>
> **Irena**

TIP

From now on, make a note of any new examples of your positive impact at work, so that you have a list that is continuously updated.

EXERCISE 16

ADDING VALUE

1. Think of a minimum of four examples in both your current and last job where you helped to add value to the organisation.

2. Include any numbers, figures or percentages to illustrate the impact. It can be approximate if you don't know the exact amount.

3. If relevant, you can also include voluntary work, placements or extra-curricular activities where you have demonstrated your worth.

TIP

Don't just rush through this exercise – take time to gather facts and information so that you have a complete picture of where you have added value, and the evidence to support it.

Company	How you added value

EXAMPLE

Company	How you added value
Jones	Developed new email policy which reduced the amount of time staff were spending on non-work related websites. Introduced e-learning which minimised time staff spent out of the office, replacing a one-day course with six 30-minute sessions.
	Negotiated new deal with stationery suppliers which achieved £500 per month in savings.
Smith	Introduced new customer worth £20k to the company. Reorganised workload of team which reduced staff headcount with savings of £25k.

Stephanie

In this chapter we have looked at how you can show an employer that you are an asset to your organisation, rather than a cost, and that in the role you are a high performer rather than a 'jobsworth'.

What you've collected together is valuable information that can be used to remind your current employer of your contribution, perhaps to justify a promotion or a pay rise. It will also be very relevant when you want to impress potential new employers. This is something that we will be focusing on in Part 7 when we develop your career marketing materials.

10 WORKING OUT WHAT YOU KNOW

Your know-how or expertise is a key part of your career offering. Some of it may be transferable to a range of different scenarios, while some will be very context-specific. For example, being an expert on tomato horticulture doesn't necessarily make you a landscape gardener, whereas IT skills such as Excel can be used in many organisations.

Interestingly, many coaching clients I work with, especially those who are in a non-specialist role, take their knowledge for granted. It's almost as though it is so embedded that they lose sight of it.

For your career capital to retain its value, your knowledge has to be continuously updated. This might mean going on top-up courses, reading journals, attending conferences or professional events. You could be the most highly qualified person in your organisation, but if you've not kept abreast of developments in your field, you could be a liability. For example who would want to employ an HR officer who doesn't know about the latest employment legislation or an administrator who can only use an old software package?

> I didn't realise at first that I was an expert in anything, but then it came up that one of my main duties is arranging exports and I guess I am very knowledge-able about this, having done it for 20 years.
>
> **Isobel**

In this chapter, we are going to capture on paper what you know. This will include looking at your key areas of knowledge and your learning and development activities, as well as your qualifications and any professional memberships. We'll also look at who you know, your non-work experiences, and hobbies and interests to discover other areas of knowledge and skills that are all part of your career capital.

Work-related qualifications

An employer will place high value on any qualifications you have achieved that are directly relevant to the job you are applying for. The fact that you had to pass an exam, provide coursework or a portfolio to achieve the qualification is evidence that you have been independently judged to have achieved a certain level of appropriate knowledge.

EXERCISE 17

YOUR PROFESSIONAL CREDIBILITY

Qualifications

Write down all of your vocationally related qualifications, such as certificates, diplomas, NVQs, vocational degrees or postgraduate training.

EXAMPLE

Professional diploma in marketing
Certificate in professional sales practice
Level 7 qualification in executive management
Degree in business studies

Rose

EXERCISE 17 (CONT.)

Professional memberships

List any memberships of professional organisations to which you belong, for example the General Medical Council or the Chartered Institute of Public Relations. Such organisations usually require members to work to certain standards and ethics. Also include any other work-related memberships that illustrate you take your professional commitments seriously, are keeping abreast of developments in the field and have contacts in your industry. Examples might include sitting on industry committees, cross-organisational working groups, research forums, quality groups or business forums.

EXAMPLE

Associate of the Chartered Institute of Personnel and Development (CIPD)
Member of the British Psychological Society
Member of the HR Charity Sector Forum
Member of local CIPD branch committee
Active member of CIPD local policy group

Clive

Training and development

Employers want to see that you have completed relevant training in the past and that your skills are up to date. If you can demonstrate that you are committed to continuous development, your career capital is likely to have greater value because it is more current.

Write down below all the training and development activities you have undertaken. Your training and development could include any of the following.

- In-house courses such as customer service, health and safety.
- External courses such as PRINCE2.
- E-learning packages such as MCSE Microsoft engineer packages.
- Extensive reading on particular subjects, for example corporate social responsibility.
- Being involved in the fast-track talent pool at work.
- Workplace coaching or mentoring.
- Distance learning.
- Attendance at conferences or seminars.
- Participation in action learning groups.
- Secondment opportunities.

EXERCISE 18

YOUR TRAINING AND DEVELOPMENT

1. Write down all your training and development activities here.

2. Highlight any areas that need updating.

EXAMPLE

Two-day course in handling workplace conflict
Assertiveness course
On-the-job training on customer service desk
Presentation skills
Leadership training course
Investors in People training
Handling disciplinary and grievance procedures
Equal opportunities
Need to update my understanding of recent legislation

Ron

Your knowledge

As well as your qualifications and training, you will have gathered an enormous amount of knowledge throughout your working life. This is just as valuable as the qualifications you have, but it's important to be specific if you want to showcase this knowledge.

Think about your current and previous jobs. Imagine yourself in the role. What kind of things do people ask your advice on? When would your input be required? What prior knowledge would a new recruit to your role be required to have? And what additional knowledge have you gained over and above what was required for a particular role?

EXERCISE 19

EXTRACTING YOUR KNOWLEDGE

For each position you have held, try to identify the knowledge you had that was important to the organisation. Examples could include:

- your technical expertise, for example management accounts
- knowledge about a particular type of product or service, for example mobile phones
- understanding of a particular industry or sector, for example local councils
- local or international knowledge, for example doing business in China
- cultural knowledge, for example working with different ethnic groups

- knowledge of systems and procedures, for example ISO quality standards
- research knowledge, for example clinical trials
- knowledge of particular customers or suppliers, for example SMEs (small and medium enterprises) or the elderly.

Write down your key areas of knowledge below.

TIP

To help you do this exercise, refer back to Exercise 12 on page 58 for your list of previous jobs.

EXAMPLE

International conference management *Service level agreements*
Sales and marketing *Public sector procurement*
Webinars *Recruitment*
Formulating business proposals *Budget management*
Chairing meetings *Performance incentives*

Andy

Non-work experiences

Any experience where you were working in a relevant environment, taking the opportunity to develop your skills and abilities, or demonstrating your willingness to work hard and contribute can be of potential interest to an employer.

For example, voluntary work is a great way to prove your work ethic, and it suggests that you have the kind of energy and community spirit that employers hope their staff will bring into the organisation with them. Some examples could include:

- organising a charity event
- internships or work placements
- helping in a friend's business
- sitting on a residents' committee
- mentoring vulnerable people
- organising the local football team.

EXERCISE 20

OTHER WORK EXPERIENCE

Write down your other experiences below.

EXAMPLE

Been helping get sponsorship for the school fête – talking to local businesses, including the garden centre, who gave us lots of plants to sell. Helped organise local campaign to fight proposed building on green belt land.

Sandra

Hobbies and interests

What hobbies or outside (non-work) interests do you have? These are definitely worth noting because they may be directly relevant to the type of job you are seeking next but it can also spark ideas that are useful for later when we look at your options. I've worked with many clients who used their outside interests as a way to transform their career. Some of them used their existing professional skills to move to companies such as arts organisations and charitable causes they felt passionately about. Others completely reinvented themselves becoming alternative therapists, fitness coaches, property developers, restaurant-owners or by setting up their own artisan business.

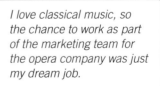

I love classical music, so the chance to work as part of the marketing team for the opera company was just my dream job.

Fran

YOUR HOBBIES AND INTERESTS

Write these below.

EXAMPLE

I'm interested in photography, computer games, cars, gadgets, iPhone apps.

Graham

Your networks

Your ability to access people, information and resources can form a key part of your career capital. If you know the key people in your industry, have relationships in place with potential customers, or know those with influence in the sector, these relationships can be used for the employer's benefit. For instance, people working in PR will be expected to have a range of suitable contacts. A sales person who already knows people who are likely to buy their product is at an advantage. Think about the people you know or who you can get access to, including:

- potential customers – individuals, groups or organisations
- key industry players, such as large organisations in your field
- relevant decision-makers, for example local councils
- political representatives, such as MPs
- those who can give you information and access to resources
- trade bodies
- prestige contacts, for example VIPs, celebrities.

Write down here the people you know and the type of contacts you have that could be of interest to a potential employer.

EXERCISE 22

YOUR NETWORKS

Write these below.

EXAMPLE

Procurement manager at ZYS
Journalist with local paper
Rachel who sits on the board of trustees
Ben at the FSB
Jane who does the training
Ryan at the software company

Adrian

ADDITIONAL INFORMATION

Is there anything else you believe you can offer that would be of interest to a potential employer? For example:

- publications, blogs, articles that you have written
- conference presentations you have given
- languages that you speak
- attendance on influential committees.

EXAMPLE

I write a weekly blog on green issues and have stood as a local councillor.

Gary

Understanding your career capital

In Part 3 we have looked in detail at the many elements that comprise your career capital.

Almost every client I have ever worked with has failed to appreciate the depth and breadth of their career capital. If you don't know the value of what you've got, you are in danger of underselling yourself.

It is highly probable that your existing manager is unaware of many of the things you can offer. If there are areas of skill and knowledge that you would like to use more of, then it is worth speaking with them to discuss possibilities. I remember working with a client who spoke several languages. It wasn't strictly relevant to the job she was doing, but she could see that it could be of real help when the company were arranging their international conference. They agreed and she proved to be so successful working alongside the event management team that a year later she moved to become a full member of that department.

TIP

On page 292 there is a section for you to fill in the key elements of your career capital in your Career Summary document. Turn to that page now and include the information you have collected from Part 3 so that you have an easily accessible record that you can turn to in the future.

EXERCISE 24

REFLECTING ON PART 3

In this section you have gathered together a lot of information, covering many different areas, about your career capital.

Review the following exercises:

- Exercise 14: Skills assessment (page 67)
- Exercise 15: Identifying your achievements (page 73)
- Exercise 16: Adding value (page 79)
- Exercise 17: Your professional credibility (page 82)
- Exercise 18: Your training and development (page 84)
- Exercise 19: Extracting your knowledge (page 85)
- Exercise 20: Other work experience (page 87)
- Exercise 21: Your hobbies and interests (page 88)
- Exercise 22: Your networks (page 89)
- Exercise 23: Additional information (page 90)

Now complete the following reflections exercise. The idea of this exercise is to capture any thoughts you may have about the following.

- What have you learned about yourself from this section?
- What have you found difficult?
- Have you had any other thoughts or ideas during these exercises?
- Actions for you to take.

My reflections on what I can offer

Action points

EXAMPLE

When I looked at my career capital I must admit I felt quite impressed. There was more there than I thought there was.

I'd forgotten that I have a lot of knowledge about working with vulnerable people through my work with social services. It is very relevant for helping me deal with difficult customers in my current job because a lot of it was about handling conflict in a very helpful way.

Action points

1. *Remind myself of all the things I have to offer as a confidence boost.*

2. *Use the information gained from this section when writing my CV and for interview.*

3. *Investigate courses to develop my skills further.*

Sharon

We will revisit this reflections exercise later when we look back on your career coaching journey in Exercise 49 on page 295.

All about you

So far we've looked at your current career situation, your personal and work history, and your career capital.

In Part 4, we are going to be finding out more about your personality and behaviours in the workplace. We are also going to gather feedback from your friends and colleagues to see how other people view you.

Whether you like it or not, a prospective employer makes a judgement about the kind of person they think you are, and whether you are a good fit for their organisation. If you are aware of your own workstyle you can actively seek organisations that work in a complementary way to your own approach.

In this section we will:

■ look at your personality type and how this affects your career

■ discover what workstyle suits you

■ get some feedback on how others see you

11 YOUR WORK-STYLE

There are certain personal traits and behaviours that every employer will want their staff to have, regardless of the role. These include:

- reliability
- honesty
- flexibility
- energy
- being hardworking
- being a team player
- showing initiative
- having a customer focus
- paying attention to standards.

However, there are a number of other factors that will come into play when employers are considering your suitability for their organisation. These include:

- any personality traits considered to be helpful in a specific job
- whether your behaviour is consistent with a particular organisational culture
- whether you will work in a complementary way with others.

In these respects, there is no right or wrong type of personality. What is considered 'right' is simply what is suitable for that particular context. An example might be the mental toughness required to be a traffic warden or the patience of a care assistant, but not necessarily vice versa.

Your personality

Some employers use personality-type questionnaires to help them choose staff with the behavioural traits identified by the company as necessary for effective performance in a specific role. For instance, a company might want to check whether candidates for a trainee auditor role can work in a systematic and detailed way or a salesperson is sufficiently resilient to deal with rejections.

> *I hated my last job. My boss was very fussy about how he wanted things done and I used to get quite angry that he would make such a fuss over small details and it made me feel incompetent.*
>
> **Sian**

However, when we look at personality and behaviour from an individual's perspective rather than in relation to a specific role, we can see that there are some other factors that need to be considered.

Your workstyle is likely to be broadly consistent across different jobs. If you are highly organised in one job you are likely to be equally organised in another.

However, there may also be reasons why your behaviour could change. For example, even the most socially confident extrovert may start behaving in an anxious and uncertain way if they are feeling undermined by others at work.

I'm sure there will be times when you remember feeling on top of the world in your job: bright, confident, energised and capable. There are also likely to be other times when your confidence dwindled and the things you thought you were good at seemed to evaporate.

The following exercise is based on the personality 'types' used as a basis for most of the commonly used personality questionnaires. For this exercise, deliberately look for consistencies in your workstyle across different work contexts, rather than just looking at your current role or any exceptions.

EXERCISE 25

SELF-ASSESSMENT

1. Answer the questions below as honestly as you can. There are no right or wrong answers: the questions are merely prompts to get you thinking about yourself. The purpose of the exercise is simply to help you understand more about yourself at work.

2. Provide examples where you can as evidence for your answers. You can choose from different jobs or career-related experience as you wish, but your examples must be work-related, not personal.

3. Feel free to add any other personality traits or behaviours that you think are accurate for you.

	Answers and examples
Do you like working in detail or are you more of a 'big picture' person?	
Are you a meticulous planner or are you more spontaneous?	
How comfortable are you working in high-pressure situations?	
Do you like to be the leader or the helper?	
How have you handled any failures at work, either your own or others?	
How comfortable are you talking to people you don't know?	
Do you like a set routine or do you welcome interruptions?	
How competitive are you?	
Would others describe you as more of an optimist or a pessimist?	
Do you like things to be perfect or are you happy with 'good enough'?	
How creative or artistic are you?	
Do you like to blend in at work or do you enjoy being different?	

Which do you enjoy working with the most: facts and figures; abstract concepts, practical things or people?	
Are you an original thinker? Do you like to look at new ways of doing things?	
Are you results-oriented or is the process as or, perhaps, more, important to you?	
Would other people see you as more of a 'doer', a 'thinker' or a 'people person'?	
If you manage staff, how would your staff describe your management style, for example consultative, decisive, empowering?	
Do you prefer working with things, equipment or hands-on tasks rather than intellectual or emotional challenges?	
How comfortable are you with taking risks?	
Do you like working as part of a group or team or more independently?	
How important is it for you that you are physically active in your work?	
Do you like helping or caring for people?	
Do you like working to targets and deadlines or do you prefer a looser structure?	

EXAMPLE

	Answers and examples
Do you like working in detail or are you more of a 'big picture' person?	*Big picture person. Enjoyed working on the new policies but preferred leading the discussion rather than writing the actual policies, which were cumbersome and a bit boring.* *When making a deal, I like building the relationship but I will leave others to manage the nitty gritty of the contract negotiation.*
Are you a meticulous planner or are you more spontaneous?	*I delegate a lot of the organisation to Maria who does it on my behalf. I just point her in the right direction.* *Wouldn't say I am a meticulous planner – can be a bit last minute, for example last year's conference, but it still tends to work out in the end.*
Do you like a set routine or do you welcome interruptions?	*I would get very bored if I did the same each day. Enjoy the variety. I like the unpredictability of my job, for example I think having to manage the product recall was something I did really well considering the time constraints we were under.*
How comfortable are you working in high-pressure situations?	*It was pretty stressful when we didn't know whether the company was being sold or not. I think it affected me only because it wasn't clear if I could make decisions or not. But normally I have to deal with lots of things that are pressured, for example trying to work out what went wrong with the product batch and handling the emergency recall.* ***Victoria***

Your answers provide important clues to help you identify which roles and organisations might suit you best in the future.

For instance, there is no point working in a sales-related role if you don't like working to targets, regardless of how attractive the rest of the package may sound. If you are someone who needs to work in a quiet, focused way then a busy open-plan office is not where you are likely to do your best work.

American psychologist John L. Holland developed a careers inventory which is often used by career advisers to help individuals think about suitable careers based on their workstyle and the kinds of organisations that would be compatible.

The inventory outlined below consists of six factors and I've included a sample list of jobs which, although not exclusive to each factor, are likely to be complementary to that workstyle.

Holland career inventory

Factor	Suitable jobs
Doer Realistic, practical, physical, hands-on, tool-orientated, mechanically inclined	Chef, mechanic, paramedic, police officer, vet, chiropodist, occupational therapist, hairdresser, personal trainer, conference organiser
Investigative Thinker, analytical, intellectual, scientific, explorative	Lawyer, doctor, statistician, psychologist, business analyst, laboratory technician, marine biologist, software developer, market researcher, economist
Creator Artistic, creative, original, independent, chaotic, non-conforming	Writer, advertising consultant, designer, PR professional, marketing manager, inventor, photographer, musician, animator, film-maker
Social Helper, co-operative, supporting, helping, healing/nurturing	Nurse, therapist, charity worker, social worker, teacher, receptionist, mediator, customer service adviser, coach, aid worker
Enterprising Competitive environments, leadership, persuading, selling, dominating, status, persuader	Sales executive, retail professional, investment banker, management consultant, publisher, politician, journalist, estate agent, business strategist, entrepreneur
Organiser Conventional, detail-orientated, organised, attention to detail, status	Proofreader, technical writer, quality control officer, computer programmer, auditor, logistics professional, company secretary, accountant, town planner, clinical researcher

Based on the **Holland Codes** *by John L. Holland*

YOUR PERSONALITY TYPE

1. Using your answers from Exercise 25, and reading through the Holland Career inventory on page 101, write down below which factor you think suits you the most and why.

2. Don't worry if you want to write down more than one factor. Where you are a blend of types, then you'll be pleased to know that there are many jobs that could sit in both categories; for example, an engineer could be both practical and investigative, while a nurse might fit with both the realistic and social categories.

3. Where one factor is clearly more dominant, this inventory can be a helpful steer for the kinds of jobs to investigate.

My work personality

Company style

Your compatibility with a specific role will also of course be influenced by the particular team, organisation and manager with whom you are working. Each organisation has its own culture and your manager will very much dictate how they want things done. For instance, if your manager is a stickler for detail, you will be required to work with high attention to detail regardless of whether the job function usually requires it or not.

It's also worth remembering that organisations also have their own distinctive personality. They will have a particular way of working, an expectation about what they think is the right way to do things and therefore what they demand of you.

Here are just a few examples of different types of organisational culture.

Type of organisation	Explanation	Job example
Bureaucratic	Importance of following processes, rules, procedures, paperwork	Civil service, organisations in heavily regulated industries
Altruistic	Focus on a higher value than monetary gain	Charity organisation
Entrepreneurial	Innovative, risk-taking, quick to act on opportunities, dynamic	Business start-up
Expert culture	Where knowledge is prized	University or legal firm
Task culture	Project-based, action-oriented	Manufacturing, farming
Power culture	Where decisions are made either by one person or a few key players	Family business
Creative	Where ideas, originality, aesthetics are important	Advertising, arts organisations
Reward culture	Where staff are rewarded for performance rather than length of service	Sales-driven organisations, the City
Strategic	Focus on longer-term objectives, research and development, planning	Think tanks, government departments
Short-term focus	Where product or service has a short shelf life so speed is of the essence, or temporary organisations set up for a particular task	High-street fashion, crisis helplines

EXERCISE 27

WHAT SUITS YOU?

Write down in the box the type of organisation you think would most complement your workstyle.

You might also think about organisations where you have worked in the past that you loved or loathed, and which organisational culture best describes them.

This information will be useful when you come to write your Career Action Plan later in Part 9.

My preferred type of organisation

Your personality and behaviour at work is such a key factor in your career success that it is important that we look at ways to validate your self-assessment.

In the next chapter you will be asking people you know to provide input to help check those self-perceptions.

12 FEEDBACK

When you were compiling your history and looking at your world back in Chapter 2, we knew we were looking at a very subjective world. It can be very tricky to be completely objective and there is sometimes a mismatch between how we see ourselves and how others see us. You may be full of doubts but other people may see a confident person. You may be worried that you are coming over as too pushy, when in fact others see someone who lacks assertiveness.

How others see you

In your career you are constantly being judged on your capabilities, behaviours and personality, both in your current job and any new jobs you apply for. It is essential that you understand what other people can see. Sensitive though it can sometimes be, obtaining objective feedback from others is by far the best way to do this. It will help:

- build your confidence in the things you are good at
- verify what you believe you have to offer a potential employer
- provide additional information that you may have missed
- identify any shortfalls that may emerge
- advise on how you might bridge any gaps
- provide a benchmark for how you compare with others.

In order to do this, we are going to use a process commonly used in business called a '360-degree appraisal'. It is basically a feedback exercise where you choose people who know you to comment on what you do well in the workplace and what you could do better and see if they have any advice. Most people are only too happy to offer their opinion if asked. Their view will be a subjective one as people will see you in very different lights and know you under different circumstances. You only need to think about previous jobs that you either loved or hated to see that one would have brought out your best qualities, another the worst.

However, it is likely that there will be some common themes that come up again and again and which are likely to be part of a shared perception that other people have about you wherever you are. So let's find out what they are.

360 DEGREES

The aim of this exercise is to obtain feedback from people you know about your positive skills and traits, as well as the areas that need development.

1. Collect together any appraisal reports, feedback, work emails, etc. in which someone is giving you feedback on your work-related performance, your behaviour or personal qualities. It doesn't matter whether you agree with it or not – just collect it together.

2. Write a list of people who you are comfortable to approach for feedback, and who have known you in a work context. This could include managers, colleagues, trainers, customers. Aim for a minimum of four people, with at least one being someone who has managed you or who is in a more senior position than you.

TIP

Choose people who you think will give you honest but constructive feedback.

3. Explain that you are seeking personal feedback to help you in your career development and ask whether they would be willing to arrange a time to answer some questions. Ideally they will be prepared to meet with you to discuss this because these discussions are always better face to face. However, if they are not able to meet you, you can send them the questions by email or talk to them on the phone.

TIP

You can also choose to ask family and friends the same questions. Although there will be differences in your work and home behaviours, they may have another interesting perspective, especially if you frequently have conversations with them about what is happening at work.

Ask them the following questions.

How would you describe me?

What do you think I'm good at?

What areas should I work on and why?

Have you any advice about what I could do to develop my career?

TIP

You may also want to check if the feedback agrees with your self-assessments in Exercises 25, 26 and 27.

Make sure you completely understand what is being said, and ask for clarification if there is anything about which you are unsure. Ask them to give examples wherever they can of what you do well and the areas that require attention. Stay open-minded to what they are saying because even if you don't agree with them, it's important for you to know where your perceptions are different from theirs and possibly the areas you need to work on.

EXAMPLE FEEDBACK: FROM YOUR EX-MANAGER

How would you describe me?

Positives: Hard-working, conscientious, perfectionist, trustworthy, expert, reliable, clever, invaluable in a team, sets the standard, gets the job done.

Negatives: bit hard-going sometimes, serious, can be argumentative, sometimes inflexible, hard taskmaster – which can be demotivating – very challenging, likes things to be done in a particular way.

What do you think I'm good at?

You are very detail-oriented. I can always expect your work to be done thoroughly and well, without mistakes, for example I've never had to make many corrections to your work so I feel I can trust you to get it right. Your work on the new website was excellent.

What areas should I work on and why?

You are quite hard on yourself, which means you have very high expectations of yourself and others. This means that you can get disappointed and frustrated when things don't go according to plan. Managing your personal emotions when dealing with practical problems will help others see you as the problem-solver, rather than someone who seems overwhelmed – your frustration with the web development company meant we had to calm you down.

Have you any advice on what I could do to develop my career?

Give yourself room for manoeuvre rather than trapping yourself and others. Use positive encouragement rather than the language of fear, such as telling people where they are on track rather than just talking about how much they still have to do.

Pete

Once you have gathered the information from all your feedback discussions, collate them together and summarise them all below or on a separate piece of paper.

What positive comments did you receive?

What do you need to work on and how will you do it?

Were there any surprises?

Are there any implications for what you or others see as your career capital or workstyle?

What else have you learned from this exercise?

EXAMPLE

What positive comments did you receive?

Everyone thought I was a friendly person and well mannered. They thought that I could talk to anyone and was very charming. That I looked good and was very professional. They thought I was a very good representative for the company.

What do you need to work on and how will you do it?

Being more assertive with people who were problematic. Could be too eager to please – sometimes needed to say no earlier. Needed to be able to show a tougher edge if want to progress in career. Will talk to HR for advice.

Were there any surprises?

I thought my people skills were great but other people didn't feel that I was good at handling conflict. I think they are wrong but this is clearly a perception that more than one person had.

Are there any implications for what you or others see as your career capital or workstyle?

There is a mismatch at the moment until I can prove that I can handle conflict and be decisive.

What else have you learned from this exercise?

That being likeable isn't enough. I need to demonstrate toughness. So I need to look out for opportunities to do that.

Gina

We will revisit this exercise when we create your Career Summary document in Part 9.

We saw in Part 1 how important our self-perceptions are in terms of our career. In this chapter we have confronted how far those perceptions match those of others. Feedback will be useful throughout your career to ensure you are on the right track and advise you how to get to your destination even more quickly. You just need to ask!

In Part 4 we have looked at your workstyle and the type of organisation that might suit you best, and sought feedback from others that may have supported or even challenged some of your self- perceptions.

You will find this very useful when you come to set your career goals.

REFLECTING ON PART 4

Review the following exercises:

- Exercise 25: Self-assessment (page 97)
- Exercise 26: Your personality type (page 102)
- Exercise 27: What suits you? (page 104)
- Exercise 28: 360 degrees (page 107)

Now let's take a moment to capture any other thoughts, ideas or information that have surfaced. Think about the following, for example.

- What has been helpful to you in this section?
- What emotions have you felt while working on this section and why?
- Any other comments.
- Any actions to be taken.

My reflections on my personality and workstyle

Action points

EXAMPLE

I was taken aback by the feedback exercise. While there were some things I knew, for example that I was a very task-orientated person and great at getting the job done, I hadn't realised that people saw me as quite so ruthless. I don't suffer fools gladly and I guess that is why I have always been very comfortable working in quite aggressive commercial organisations. I think a slow-paced organisation or 'ditherers' would irritate me. Got some good useful advice, I think, about my need to move from a 'cracking the whip' style to a more leadership approach, especially if I want to move into more strategic roles.

Action points

1. *Ask HR if they can arrange coaching or mentoring for me to develop my people management expertise.*

2. *Pay more attention at work to building good relationships.*

3. *Next career move must be in a fast-paced, commercial organisation.*

Graham

We will revisit this reflections exercise when we look back on your career coaching journey in Part 9.

Well done for all your hard work so far – we've come a long way. You've examined your career from every angle, from both current and historical perspectives, internally and externally, with a microscope and with 360-degree panoramic vision. It will have provided you with the firm foundations you need to start thinking about your future career journey.

PART 5

Options and decisions

From here onwards, the career coaching is going to be very future-focused as we start to look at your options and make decisions.

However, you may have found that some positive changes have already started to take place. You may have spoken to your boss, arranged some personal development or started applying for a new role. You may have had a meeting with a business contact that resulted in a job interview or made some decisions about the future.

Whether or not things have already started to change for you, the career management strategies in this section will show you how to make informed career decisions and clarify your goals for the future.

In this section we will:

■ visualise what you would like your future to be

■ understand your options

■ generate job ideas

■ reality-check your options

■ confirm your career decisions

13 SEE THE FUTURE

In this chapter you are going to create a clear picture in your head of what you want your career to look like.

This is especially important if you feel, as many people do, that your future career seems 'vague' or 'fuzzy'. If you don't know what you are looking for, then how are you going to find it?

I speak to lots of individuals in this situation who describe feeling stuck because they 'don't know what is out there'. They have been wearily trawling through recruitment adverts looking for inspiration and then been disappointed when they don't find it. Their CV will be unfocused because they are trying to cover too many job options, and when they speak to recruiters, their doubts will spark questions about whether to put them forward for the role or not. The perfect job for them might well be under their nose but they wouldn't recognise it.

Instead of looking outwards for inspiration, we first need to go inwards and build upon all of the information we have gathered so far. This chapter is going to help you do just that.

EXERCISE 30

CAREER WISH LIST

1. Before completing this exercise, take another look at the exercises in Part 1, especially Exercise 7 (page 30). Look at the things you wanted to change when we first set out on this career coaching process.
    *   Are those career desires still current for you?
    *   Do you have any new priorities?

2. From the list below, highlight those that are your current career priorities. Feel free to add as many others as you wish.

3. Refer to your key career 'I wants' from Exercise 7.

More money	Adventure	Greater appreciation
Increased responsibility	Security	Improved relationships
Greater recognition	More respect	Greater job interest
Work with new people	Greater challenge	Move sector
Promotion	More confidence	See my children more
Greater job interest	More people contact	often
More decision-making	Less people contact	Retrain in new area
Intellectual stimulation	Greater variety	Ensure skills in demand
Learning opportunities	Progression	Stop working long hours
Less stress	To feel that I'm 'growing'	Less pressure
More fun	Easier commute	Play to my strengths
Greater status	More flexibility	To be good at my job
To make a difference	Gain experience	To prove I can do it
Greater reward	Deepen expertise	To find a new job after
Specific work-space	Improve employability	redundancy
To be myself at work	Set up own business	To return to work after
More freedom	Use creativity	a career break
More travel	Use entrepreneurial	To pay the bills
More perks	skills	To feel proud
Better work/life balance	Less hours	More influence

Using visualisations

We are now going to use this career wish list as a basis on which to visualise your ideal career. Remember how powerful the picture was in Chapter 2, when you drew your world as you saw it in that moment.

Visualisations are helpful not only in bringing to the forefront important psychological information that may be hidden or unexpressed; they can also help you create the future.

It's like the rehearsal for a play or your own personal virtual reality experience. You can use it as an imaginative test lab to experiment and rehearse with different approaches and discover what works best for you. When you can clearly see your ideal scenario it becomes far easier to articulate it to others and translate it into real life.

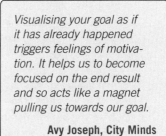

Visualising your goal as if it has already happened triggers feelings of motivation. It helps us to become focused on the end result and so acts like a magnet pulling us towards our goal.

Avy Joseph, City Minds

In the following exercise, we are going to use a visualisation that embodies your career hopes, needs and aspirations.

> *I use my visualisation before I go to a networking meeting. It reminds me of myself at my best and what I am trying to achieve.*
>
> **John**

EXERCISE 31

VISUALISING THE FUTURE

1. Read the instructions below and then close your eyes and try and blank out the world and any distractions around you. You will need to spend a minimum of 20 minutes on this exercise.

2. Think about your wish list in Exercise 30. Now imagine waking up on your perfect day at work. Visualise your whole day from the time you get up in the morning to the moment when your head rests on the pillow at night. You might want to include the following details.
    - How do you feel when you wake up? What does breakfast look like? Is there anyone else around? What do you choose to wear? How do you get to work and what is the journey like?
    - At work, what activities are you involved in? What are your interactions with other people? What have you achieved in the morning? What do you do for lunch? What do you do in the afternoon?
    - What do you do after work? What is your journey home like? What happens when you get home?

3. Create all the sights, sounds, smells and feelings associated with your perfect day at work. Immerse yourself imaginatively in the picture and enjoy every single detail. This picture is you at your best and most positive.

4. Did that feel good? Now let's make your visualisation tangible by drawing a picture of the key elements you saw and the emotions you felt. Remember, your drawing skills are completely unimportant. Try to use colour in your drawing to help your creativity flow. You can use the odd word if you need to.

Your picture

About your picture

Use your visualisations and pictures to draw out the following.

What are the most important elements of your career vision for you?

What are you doing?

How do you feel in your visualisation?

Who else is in the picture and what is your relationship with them?

What are the key differences from 'My World Picture'?

What can you do to help make your picture become a reality?

EXAMPLE

What are the most important elements of your career vision for you?

Seemed to be busy but relaxed and it felt like the work was under control.

That I was working between home and the office – and avoiding the rush hour commute. That I wasn't being bombarded with interruptions like I normally am.

What are you doing?

I was involved in meeting customers and suppliers rather than just behind the computer.

How do you feel in your visualisation?

Felt the calmness, lack of hassle both from boss and commuting.

Who else is in the picture and what is your relationship with them?

Had brief images of being interrupted by my boss which made me feel angry but then it calmed down again. Was talking to customers.

What are the key differences from 'My World Picture'?

- *Better journey into work or more flexi-working.*
- *Being able to get on with my job without interruptions.*
- *Being trusted to represent the company with customers, etc.*

What can you do to help make your picture become a reality?

- *Could talk to my boss about staggering my start times at work.*
- *Need to manage interruptions at work more effectively.*
- *Find a new job nearer to home or home-based.*
- *Volunteer to go to exhibitions and trade events.*

Erin

It is really important for you to keep hold of your vision and replay it in your head regularly, keeping it fresh and always positive. The more you practise it, the sharper the vision will become. It will help keep you focused, motivated and resilient.

TIP

Having the image on easy recall will make it easy to express clearly to others what you are like when you are at your best and what it is that you are looking for.

14 WHAT ARE MY OPTIONS?

Now you've got a clear idea of what you'd like your future to look like, we need to start thinking practically. In this chapter we will look at the options available to you and start thinking about which is the most likely route to the career vision you imagined in the last chapter.

The great news is that everyone has options! There will be opportunities right under your nose as well as further afield. There will be some that you can step right into and others that you may need to inch towards. However, whatever your career issue or circumstances may be, you will have a number of choices.Broadly speaking, there are the following options.

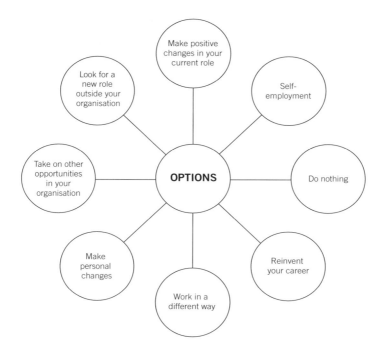

Let's look at each option in turn.

Do nothing

Of course, this is an option. The fact that you bought this book implies that you want something to change, and that doing nothing at all is perhaps not your favoured option.

Nonetheless it remains a choice that is open to you. Let's look at the pros and cons of this.

I really don't like my job. I feel sick on Sunday evening just thinking about going into work the next day and I spend most of the week just waiting for the weekend. But that's just how work is, isn't it? It's not like it would be any better elsewhere, not in today's job market.

Helen

Pros and cons of doing nothing

Pros	Cons
Takes little effort to do nothing	May take enormous effort/stress to continue status quo
It might not be the right timing	Life is too short for regrets
Others around you may not want change	Others may prefer to see you happy and fulfilled
Things could change of their own accord	Being proactive increases the likelihood of getting what you want
Low risk?	May be risks to staying where you are
Threat to financial security	Limits on potential financial gain if you stay put
Low self-esteem says that it's your fault and you don't deserve anything better	Well-being improves as a result of a move to a healthier environment
Doing nothing avoids risk of failure or rejection	Doing nothing means that others may take the opportunities you want

If this is an option that you are leaning to, it might also be worth looking again at Part 2. Have the positive things that have happened to you career-wise been a result of things just landing fortuitously in your lap or have you made them happen?

It can be tempting to sit tight and do nothing. Maybe your work will become more interesting, that elusive promotion opportunity will appear or the threatened redundancy won't happen. While 'doing nothing' may superficially seem a safe option, it is in fact the most risky. Being passive in your career makes you vulnerable because you become reliant on luck or certain key people who may or may not give you what you want. Creating options for yourself and improving your employability will help you feel psychologically far more in control. You will have insured yourself against risks and be better positioned to take roles that are right for you rather than just what happens to be available. This is especially important if your current work situation is a stressful one.

Make positive changes in your current role

This is an option that is often overlooked, mainly because people are often nervous about what they see as rocking the boat with their current employer. However, there are lots of ways in which you may be able to enhance or modify your current job to more closely match what you need, and sometimes a subtle change can make a big difference. You could, for instance:

- talk to your manager and/or HR about your career development
- ask for opportunities that stretch your capabilities
- request a pay rise
- make sure you get credit or recognition for your work
- talk to your boss if the workload is too much
- be more assertive with your manager and/or colleagues
- manage your time more efficiently
- write a blog, organise an event or join a project group
- spend some time with other departments
- undertake in-house training or train others
- take control over your work/life balance
- ask for a coach or mentor – or mentor someone else.

I asked my manager what I could do to improve my promotion prospects and she was very supportive and suggested that I needed to get some budget management experience so we agreed that I would spend an afternoon with the finance department. I've now been delegated the monthly accounts and I feel much more confident. My manager has also started delegating me other things now that she knows I want to progress my career, so I feel like I'm learning again.

Linda

Remember that it is in an employer's interest to keep their current staff motivated and engaged as they are more likely to perform better at work. Good staff are hard to find and expensive to recruit and train, so it makes financial sense for an employer to make an effort to retain the staff they want to keep.

125

However, if you are asking for something that requires additional resources, do make sure that you can show how the organisation will benefit, if you want them to agree to it. For instance, they are unlikely to fund an expensive management development course if it is not relevant to your job or they think you will leave as soon as you have completed it. They will want to see a return on their investment.

Take on other opportunities in your organisation

This could be a promotion as you step into your boss's shoes but it's not the only route for career development within your organisation.

> *I was fed up working as a retail floor manager and thinking about changing career entirely. When the training job at Head Office came along, I pulled out all the stops to make sure I got it. I now feel like I've got my motivation back.*
>
> **George**

Flatter management structures and the greater emphasis on collaborative working and knowledge sharing means fewer management levels as organisations replace some of the old command and control hierarchies with a more agile project team approach. As there are reduced promotion opportunities it can become more challenging to progress rung by rung up an internal career ladder. If you are facing a career logjam at work where the upward career paths seem to have fallen away, this doesn't mean that you have to put your career development on hold, you may just need to consider your career path in a more 360 degrees way and be proactive in carving out learning opportunities for yourself.

In this situation it is perhaps more helpful to reimagine your career in the shape of a 'career lattice' rather than an upwards stairway. This is more of a multi-directional career journey which may include a promotion but also lateral moves, different ways of working and even downward shifts at certain times of life where you for instance want to take a career break, study for a degree, care for family members or as a gentle ramp towards retirement.

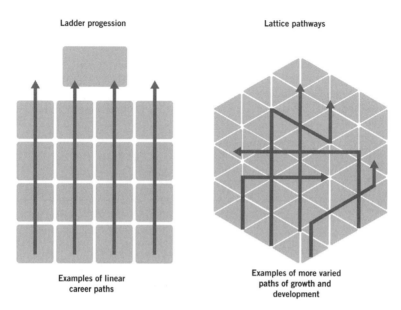

Ladder progession

Lattice pathways

Examples of linear career paths

Examples of more varied paths of growth and development

Cathy Benko and Molly Anderson, The Corporate Lattice: Achieving High Performance in the Changing World of Work

Opportunities at work could include going on a secondment, participating in a project, suggesting a research task or quality initiative, arranging a sideways shift or looking for a 'stretch' role that enables you to acquire new skills. Gaining experience with another side of the business, spending time with customers or suppliers, taking on training or mentoring of others, these are all great ways to develop your career capital, enhance your career agility, and position you for a wider range of career possibilities both within your organisation and outside.

If you don't create new opportunities within the confines of your 'day job', they may never come your way.

Hermina Ibarra, Act Like a Leader, Think Like a Leader

There are also many advantages to continuing your career with your current employer.

- Familiarity with the organisation means that an internal move is relatively low-risk compared with an external move.
- Your legal continuity of service and accrued employee rights are preserved.
- You are already likely to have some relationships in place that will help you.

- You can fully explore what the job entails before you accept.
- It looks good on your CV to show that you have been entrusted with different roles within the organisation, especially if they are promotions.
- You can try new things and develop your capabilities but within the comfort of a known environment.
- If you have been with your employer a long time then exposure to different roles in the organisation can be used to show any future recruiters that you are adaptable.
- It can be a stepping stone that takes you closer to an external role that you would otherwise be unable to step straight into.

TIP

If you are looking for a job move, it is always worth exploring what may be available internally. Too often employees hand in their notice without even considering what might be on offer.

Look for a new role outside your organisation

There may be lots of good reasons why you are looking externally for your next role. They could include:

- threat of redundancy
- limited opportunities
- unhappy workplace relationships
- boredom or disenchantment
- appeal of a fresh challenge
- being underpaid
- wanting to use different skills and expertise
- feeling unrecognised or undervalued
- being overworked
- poor management
- wanting a new career direction
- changes in personal circumstances.

You may decide to look for a similar role, something related to what you've been doing, or a complete career reinvention. It is very important that if you are looking for a new job then you are very clear about what you want and why, otherwise there is a danger that you drift into something similar or something unsuitable just because it's available rather than right for you.

> *I was going from sales account job to sales account job, moaning about my job and the people and just generally being really frustrated, fed up and cynical about work. It was only when I took a step back and considered that, although sales was the only thing I had ever done, I really didn't enjoy working in that highly pressured sales environment. I took a job instead in customer relationship management and immediately felt more comfortable and have done really well ever since. Why didn't I work that out earlier?*
>
> **Sophia**

Reflecting on your career journey to date, if you find that you have had several unhappy work experiences, then it's worth considering whether you might inadvertently be contributing to this. It might be a result of faulty choices, a mismatch in expectations, or that your interpersonal skills are hindered by low self-confidence.

In which case, it is better to sort out these issues rather than assume that the next job might be better – it probably won't. Working on your personal development, maybe with a career coach or counsellor, is likely to be of far more help than simply changing jobs.

Work in a different way

You may want to continue using your core skills, experience and knowledge, but deliver these in a different way. Options include:

- changing your working hours
- working in a job share
- having a portfolio career where you work in a number of different roles
- doing voluntary work
- combining work and study
- working from home
- working seasonally or just in term-time
- working on a project basis or in temporary positions.

If you are looking to make changes in *how* you work, for example working more flexibly, then you will need to convince your manager that the new arrangement can work well for both of you. For instance, persuading them to let you work from home one day a week might be easier if you can suggest that you will still be on call to answer telephone and emails but the reduced distractions will mean you are far more productive. Show how your proposed changes are a win-win and the answer is more likely to be yes.

Portfolio career

Having a portfolio career means your working week consists of different jobs. Your jobs may be similar in terms of their content or they could be completely different. A portfolio career might include a couple of part-time jobs, ad hoc projects, running your own business or unpaid roles.

I've worked with many clients with interesting combinations. Some have combined consultancy, writing, lecturing and unpaid advisory roles in the course of their working week. Others have had one job in the day and another completely different one in the evenings and at weekends as their 'side-hustle'. This included one client who was such an adept multi-tasker that his working week included working in corporate sales, running his own profitable e-commerce site and regularly undertaking ambitious property redevelopment projects.

> *I work as a teaching assistant during the day. I'm also a gym coach, secretary to a local committee and organise local nearly- new sales for toddler and baby toys.*
>
> **Julie**

Portfolio careers can be an excellent choice for those who:

- enjoy lots of variety in their working life
- like the independence of not being tied to one employer
- want to work part-time and need flexibility, such as mums returning to work
- are not interested in a corporate career, including those who want to continue working after retirement
- can use portfolio working as a stepping stone to a new career or to building their own business
- cannot find a job that brings together all their interests, skills and financial needs together in one role.

However, portfolio working requires a great deal of organisation. It can be tricky to co-ordinate and each employer will want full value in terms of your time and effort. To work successfully, you will need to put clear boundaries around each job. For instance, if you are paid by the hour for one job, you need to make sure that you are not on the phone to one of your other employers during that time. Only good jugglers should consider portfolio work.

Interim or temporary work

Another alternative way of working is taking temporary or interim work. Temporary work can cover a whole array of different working arrangements including opportunities arranged through an agency, directly with an employer or on a consultancy basis.

If you are interested in working for a particular organisation but not getting shortlisted for permanent jobs, then temporary work can be a great way to gain entry. I've coached many graduates who have successfully used temporary work to get their foot in the door and then ended up with a permanent job.

Working temporarily in a job can also give you valuable experience that you might need to apply for your next permanent job. For instance, public sector workers looking to transfer to the private sector might consider temporary work to help them in that transition.

Interim roles are usually undertaken by senior managers or subject specialists. They are brought into an organisation to complete a specific task or provide cover for a member of staff who is temporarily absent. Examples might include an organisational development consultant delivering a change management programme or a finance manager covering the post-holder's maternity leave.

Interim work is well worth considering if you like working in a variety of different settings and being able to pick and choose your assignments. Many professional interim roles pay more per day than their permanent employee equivalents but there is far less job security and fewer employee rights. Some interim roles will require you to set up your own company so that you can supply your services on a 'contractor' basis.

TIP

The short-term and task-focused basis of interim work means that it is particularly suited to those who are goal-orientated and who can hit the ground running on Day One of their assignment rather than needing time to settle in.

Many people enjoy the variety and flexibility of working in interim and temporary roles and have built successful and well-paid careers. However, in a tough economic climate, the interim and temporary job markets become more competitive than usual because many people who fail to get permanent work consider this as an option.

Reinvent your career

It is highly unlikely that your first job will be the same one from which you retire. Most people will have several career changes during their life especially now that we are all living and working for longer.

Sometimes a career change evolves naturally as your growing interest in an area finds opportunities in which to express itself. At other times it may be triggered by a redundancy, a health scare, a new baby, a milestone birthday or a change in personal circumstances, which may lead you to re-evaluate what you want for the rest of your working life. As Hermina Ibarra, author of *Working Identity* has suggested, there are many 'possible selves' you could pursue.

A career reinvention can take many forms, including:

- becoming more specialist in a particular area
- broadening your expertise to become more generalist
- becoming involved in advising, recruitment, training, coaching or quality control within your field
- researching and writing about your subject area or working for relevant bodies such as a professional institute or within academia
- using your transferable skills in a new role or sector
- retraining for a completely new career
- actively pursuing a new area of work that interests you, such as charity campaigning
- turning a hobby into a profession, for example garden design.

The ease with which you will be able to reinvent your career is likely to depend on how close the new role is to what you have been doing before. If there are gaps, then it may be more realistic to consider stepping-stone roles that will edge you closer over time to where you want to be.

Career change is at its most challenging for those who are mid-career and who may need to retrain and/or take a salary drop. In this instance, you need to consider very carefully whether this is financially viable and how likely it is that a prospective employer will hire a 'mature novice' in this field. Even with age discrimination legislation, late entrants to some professions, for example medicine or law, will find it more difficult at a later stage of life. However, there are some career change options where 'life experience' is a positive advantage, such as coaching, consultancy or working with vulnerable people.

The ageing workforce and reduced pensions mean that we are all much likely to be working for longer. Lynda Gratton in her book *The 100-Year Life* predicts that not only will it become routine for us to work into our 70s and 80s but that 're-creation will be more important than recreation'.

People will want and need to explore different professional identities prompted by longer work lives and the fast-paced technological changes that continually reconfigure the job market. Career change will become an even more regular feature in peoples' careers and an essential career management skill.

Self-employment

The option to work for yourself may be appealing to you. There are a number of different ways you can go about this.

- Work freelance as a sole trader, marketing and delivering your services directly to potential customers.
- Work as a sub-contractor for a company who are managing the relationship with the employer.
- Undertake work as part of the 'gig economy' which refers to tasks or piecemeal work taken on by freelancers via online platforms such as TaskRabbit or Uber.
- Create your own business to sell a service or product.
- Take over an existing business.
- Buy a franchise and run your own business under an established brand.

The McKinsey Global Institute (MGI) estimates the independent workforce is some 162 million people, up to 30% of the working-age population across the United States and much of Europe. Almost five million people in the UK are employed in this way.

Self-employment can be very rewarding. However, any new business venture brings a different set of challenges from those of being an employee.

While it offers much greater independence and potentially greater rewards, running your own business is riskier, more pressured and is likely to take you into areas that are outside your comfort zone. For instance, regardless of your particular expertise, you are going to have to become involved in selling. No product or service just sells itself. If you don't have a sales background, acquiring these skills can be quite a steep learning curve. You will also have to deal with issues that as an employee other people did for you: accounts, invoicing, VAT, IT systems, marketing, premises management, legislation … the list goes on!

Yet many people (including myself!), once they have started their own business, never want to go back.

TIP

There is more information about self-employment on pages 247–250.

Make personal changes

As we've found already, your career does not exist in isolation from the rest of your life. It may be that there are changes which you can make outside of the workplace that could have a positive impact on your career. Examples could include:

- changing childcare arrangements to something that works better
- addressing high stress levels through counselling, mindfulness, exercise etc
- asking for more support from your partner
- taking up a creative hobby to express yourself outside work
- leaving earlier to miss the traffic
- updating your image to change perceptions at work.

You may remember that we looked at some of these practicalities in Chapter 3 on work/life balance. Your answers to Exercise 4 (page 21) will form one of your career goals in your Career Action Plan in Part 9 (page 283).

As you can see from this chapter, there are lots of options for you to consider, so let's capture your initial thoughts about which are the most appealing to you.

EXERCISE 32

INTERESTING OPTIONS

1. Think of your career wish list (Exercise 30, page 116), and your future career picture (Exercise 31, page 118).

2. Consider all the options in this chapter and feel free to bring in any others you think are relevant. Which options do you think offer the best route to achieving your career vision?

3. Are there options that can act as useful stepping stones to get you closer even if they don't take you the whole way?

4. If you are currently working, could there be any possibilities within your current organisation?

5. Write your answers on the next page.

Options

> **EXAMPLE**
>
> *Definitely interested in looking for a new role focused on corporate social responsibility. It's probably not going to happen in my current organisation as it's too removed from what I am doing now, although I wonder if I could get involved with the in-house employee volunteering scheme which has lacked some energy. Maybe I could suggest a project and organise it as this would give me very good experience and bring me into contact with the external relations team who handle CSR. If I build some relationships there maybe they would consider me for a role within their team. At the very least, spending some time with them would be a helpful learning experience to put on my CV when I start applying for junior CSR type roles.*
>
> ***Meera***

In this chapter we've covered a lot of options available to you, many of which could help you on your way to your next career move and your longer-term career strategy.

At this point, if you have a good idea of exactly what you want your next role to be, you can go straight to Chapter 16 on page 142 to look at reality-testing.

However, if you are unsure about what job you want, perhaps because you are considering a career reinvention, the next chapter is going to help you generate job ideas for you to consider.

15 GENERATING IDEAS

We have already looked in depth at your career capital and also your workstyle, so you are likely to have a sense of what you are good at, what you enjoy and the way you like to work. If you are thinking about moving sectors or roles, this chapter will show you how to generate ideas for potential jobs.

> ## TIP
>
> Exploring ideas can take time, so enjoy your research and take this opportunity to delve into areas you may not have considered before.

Careers information resources

There are so many potential fields for you to choose from that sometimes it can feel a bit daunting. The list below indicates the main headings for more than 800 different job profiles that are freely available for you to look at on the website https://nationalcareersservice.direct.gov.uk with professions ranging from archivist to zoologist. This resource will tell you the about the skills and qualifications needed to get into each job, the pay, prospects and what the work will be like.

Administrative and clerical
Alternative therapies
Animals, plants and land
Arts, crafts and design
Catering services
Construction
Legal services
Maintenance, service and repair
Management and planning
Manufacturing and engineering
Marketing, selling and advertising

Medical technology
Medicine and nursing
Performing arts, broadcast and media
Education and training
Environmental sciences
Financial services
General and personal services
Information management
Information technology
Publishing and journalism

Retail sales and customer service
Science and research
Security and uniformed services
Social services

Sport, leisure and tourism
Storage, dispatching and delivery
Transport

Pick the ones that are of interest to you and then find out more detailed information on the different roles available in these fields. The site also has a skills questionnaire that will suggest some occupations based on your answers.

The graduate careers site www.prospects.ac.uk has a list of career ideas for those studying for different degrees.

TIP

Don't get too stuck on job titles as these can vary widely. Focus more on the main activities of the role and the type of organisation or sector.

Interesting organisations

If there is a particular organisation or type of organisation that appeals to you, for example media or a charity, go directly to the websites of companies operating in this field to find out more about the type of positions they have.

TIP

Many large companies have a careers section on their website with lots of useful information, including vacancies, job descriptions, organisation charts and case studies. For example, the BBC careers website includes lots of articles and videos about different roles, entry schemes and vacancies within the BBC.

The company may also have a social media site on Facebook or LinkedIn where you can find out more about the company, get regular information updates and participate in online discussions.

Once you start looking at organisations that appeal, you will discover the different capacities in which they employ people. You can then decide whether any of them are job roles that you would be interested in pursuing further.

If you know anyone who works for the organisation, ask them to keep you updated if any opportunities arise.

Ask people you know

Share with people the key elements of your career capital and your career vision. Talk about your practical skills and experience and then describe, from your career picture, the type of work activities and organisations you are interested in for the future. Ask for their advice and suggestions. Encourage as many contributions as you can – family, friends, contacts, colleagues. Reject nothing at this stage. Other people can have great ideas and spark some new ideas of your own.

Recruitment sites

There are thousands of different possibilities listed on recruitment websites. While there's probably too much information to start trawling through randomly looking for career inspiration, the keyword search function on each database can be very helpful.

For example, you might be interested in marketing but also music. Type in these as a keyword combination in the search bar, adding any relevant filters such as salary range or location and see what the database comes up with as a suitable job. It's like a keyword job lucky dip and is great for generating job ideas. If you find something you like, use the job title to explore other jobs in the same field. Go onto the business networking site LinkedIn to find individuals with similar job titles to look at their profiles to find out more about their job and the career paths they took to get there.

> *I kept highlighting jobs that were animal related because I love my dogs. My background is IT so I wasn't going to retrain to be a vet but it did make me think that I could work for an organisation that was animal related. I'm now working in IT for a big animal welfare charity and am loving it.*
>
> **Ian**

Equally look at jobs that you think sound interesting. It doesn't matter what the job title is. What is it about each of these jobs that appeals to you? Are there some common themes that link the jobs together such as working in a role connected with science or working for social justice? Then use these themes as keywords in the website's job search function along with some of your existing core skills to see what possibilities might emerge, for example "sports, marketing, international".

If you want to know more about a range of roles available within a specialist function or sector, then try websites that are more niche such as www.totallylegal.com for legal jobs or www.gaapweb.com for finance professionals.

> # TIP
>
> Job fairs are held across the country and throughout the year; these are worth attending as they give you the opportunity to talk directly to recruitment teams from many different organisations and find out more about the opportunities that are available.

Online forums and resources

There are thousands of online forums where you can participate in career discussions. This includes LinkedIn groups for particular sectors or types of jobs. There are many community discussion portals such as those at *The Guardian* careers website, www.theguardian.com/careers. It features articles, videos and podcasts on a whole range of career-related matters including regular interactive online Q&A forums with industry experts advising on what it is like to work in a particular field and how to get your foot in the door. Many professional associations will have their own online networks, as well as niche groups such as www.recruitforspouses.co.uk who specialise in the recruitment of those with partners serving in the military. These are great resources for generating career ideas and connecting with people who can give you advice.

EXERCISE 33

YOUR IDEAS

1. Spontaneously write down all the job ideas that interest you – aim for a minimum of six. They may be ideas that you have been thinking of for a while, prompted by this chapter and your investigations, or suggested by other people.

2. Capture your ideas as a mind-map as in the example on page 141, or as a list or diagram.

3. Don't exclude anything at this stage.

4. From your list, decide which ones are the most appealing. Circle these or highlight them, and start with these when you come to the next stage of your research – in Chapter 16.

Your ideas

EXAMPLE

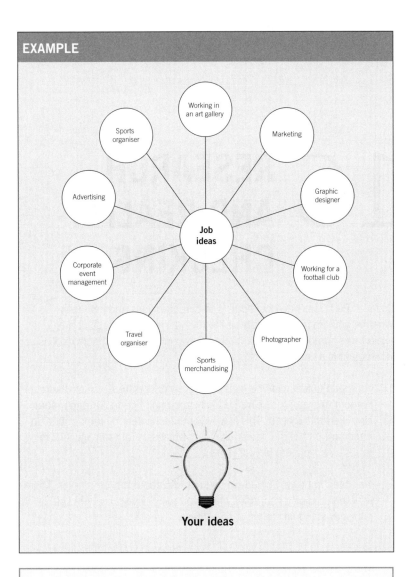

Your ideas

TIP

If you are still finding it difficult to either generate ideas or to
process the information available, you will find it helpful to talk to
a careers professional such as a career coach or careers adviser.
They can signpost you to relevant career ideas and help you gauge
their suitability.

In the next chapter we are going to look more closely at your ideas and then
test their suitability for you.

16 RESEARCH AND REALITY-CHECKING

So far in Part 5 we have looked at your career options and job ideas. Whether you are fairly clear about the role you want to pursue or are exploring a number of options, there are two important elements to consider when making a career choice.

1. You need to feel genuine passion, energy and enthusiasm for the role. Without this your job search is likely to be half-hearted and therefore less likely to succeed. This is why your ideal career picture is such an important part of the career coaching process. (Turn to page 119 to refresh your picture in your mind.)

2. You need to be very clued-up and realistic about the job market. There is no point applying for roles which you might love but where you currently stand little chance of success.

> *I would have thought twice about being a sound engineer if I'd realised what working freelance involved. There is no security. I'm having to work away from home all the time. It's not what I wanted.*
>
> **Ben**

Even if the job you want is currently out of reach, don't be disheartened. If you are not ready to jump into it yet, look for a stepping-stone role that will take you closer.

Perhaps undertaking some additional training or obtaining some more experience would help you get there quicker. Alternatively, there may be another career route that will give you what you want career-wise, but be easier to achieve. There is no point making it more difficult than it has to be.

In this chapter we are going to look at the options and ideas that interest you and then reality-check them, because you need to know that what you are aiming for is realistic.

Beware assumptions!

Many clients come to career coaching because they have been disappointed at the lack of success in their job applications. Very often it's because they have simply misunderstood the employer's requirements and are applying for roles for which they are unsuitable. For instance, I have talked to several people who believe that because they are a manager in one organisation they can be a manager in *any* organisation. While management is a transferable skill, it does not in itself make you the right candidate for every management job. There will be a whole range of other selection criteria that you will need to satisfy.

If you have been surprised to be rejected for a job for which you thought you were the ideal candidate, the chances are that your application made some false assumptions about what you thought the employer wanted to hear.

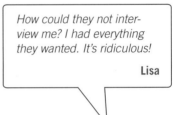

How could they not interview me? I had everything they wanted. It's ridiculous!

Lisa

It is essential that you do your research properly now rather than making short-cut assumptions as it will save you an awful lot of time, energy and frustration later when you come to implement your Career Action Plan.

What you need to find out

Whatever option you are interested in, you need to research the following.

- The market demand for this type of role, now and for the future.
- Typical entry routes into the job and progression opportunities.
- Qualifications and training requirements.
- What the job involves on a day-to-day basis.
- Salary information.
- Selection criteria used by employers to recruit candidates.
- Feedback from recruiters/employers on your suitability.
- Information about organisations that recruit for these roles.
- Inside information from those who currently work in the role or organisation in which you are interested.
- Any personal factors or circumstances that could help or hinder in this role.

How to access this information

Job market demand

When you are making a choice about your next career move, it's important to check out whether this is a market where demand is likely to continue to be healthy or whether it may be due to dwindle.

Don't rely on recruitment websites alone to try to assess the demand. You may see lots of relevant jobs listed on a website but it is common for the same job to be advertised several times on websites by different agencies but labelled differently. There are also significant regional differences as the local job market in, for instance, Manchester is likely to be different from rural Devon.

In terms of longer-term trends, we know that the ageing population means increased demand for products and services targeted for this group. We also know that data science, artificial intelligence, automation, virtual and augmented reality are huge areas of growth. Carl Frey of Oxford University estimates that over 40% of jobs are likely to be replaced by computers by 2030 with professional jobs such as auditing, legal services, medical and middle management increasingly being automated.

There will still be lots of jobs where a human operator is far more preferable. For instance would you want a robot to cut your hair or create your advertising campaign? Creativity, empathy, judgement, innovation, nuanced thinking and emotional intelligence are unlikely as yet to be outsourced to a machine. However, if you are currently a taxi driver or car salesman then it's worth thinking now about how the imminent arrival of driverless cars could affect your business.

You can find lots of information on the internet about labour market trends for different sectors or regions, simply type in 'trends legal sector' or 'labour market London' for example to find reports and articles from professional associations, recruitment companies, sector skills councils, trade journals, etc, which will give you a temperature check on the demand for certain roles or sectors you may be interested in and projected trends for the future.

Using job adverts

You may feel you have looked at lots of job adverts during your research in Chapter 15. But let's look at them closely to find out how well they match what you want and how easy it might be for you to persuade an employer that you have everything they need.

INTERPRETING JOB ADVERTS

1. Find three to four job adverts for **each** of the kind of roles you are interested in applying for.

2. Look very closely at the job details from the different job ads you have gathered and answer the following questions for each role option.

Role option 1

What activities do the jobs have in common?

Is the job what you expected it to be?

What are the differences between the jobs?

Which is more appealing to you and why?

What are the selection criteria? Are you a good match?

Are there any gaps? If so, is there anything you can do to bridge them?

Role option 2

What activities do the jobs have in common?

Is the job what you expected it to be?

What are the differences between the jobs?

Which is more appealing to you and why?

What are the selection criteria? Are you a good match?

Are there any gaps? If so, is there anything you can do to bridge them?

EXAMPLE

Job title: Charity Fundraiser

This role involves:
- developing the major donor/corporate fundraising strategic plan
- delivery and implementation of that plan against targets
- producing leaflets, reports, films for donor meetings
- soliciting large donations (£25,000+) and developing the patron programme
- liaising with patrons, organising events, receptions, briefings, discussions, etc
- identifying new prospects from our databases and outside sources.

Person specification:
- five years' fundraising experience, including at least three years in major donor fundraising or client liaison experience
- proven track record in developing major donor relationships
- demonstrable strategic and creative approach to developing fundraising opportunities

- experience of making outstanding presentations, networking, negotiation and influencing others
- excellent interpersonal skills and the ability to communicate, both orally and in writing, at all levels
- proven events experience.

What activities do the jobs have in common?

Devising campaign plans and organisation, meeting donation targets, events organisation, donor relationships.

Is the job what you expected it to be?

Mostly. Lots of emphasis on finding new prospects.

What are the differences between the jobs?

Some are more focused on individual patrons, others looking for corporate donors or government/lottery support. Jobs seemed to be quite different depending on who they were approaching for money.

Which is more appealing to you and why?

I think I would feel more comfortable working with corporate donors as this is more my background. I understand what organisations are looking for in terms of their corporate social responsibility aims.

What are the selection criteria? Are you a good match?

I match quite a few of the things they are looking for. Particularly the events organisation, making presentations, writing leaflets and other communications. I think I have great experience in this and I have done this for charities before. However, I haven't worked specifically in fundraising.

Are there any gaps? If so, is there anything you can do to bridge them?

I don't have the substantial experience of working solely in fundraising. However, I think I would be very good at it. If I could find myself a role working as an assistant in a fundraising department I could learn how to devise and organise a fundraising campaign plan and I think I would very quickly prove myself.

Nicky

If you can satisfy a minimum of 95% of the criteria on the job ad and provide examples to prove it, this is likely to be a good match. Although, of course, this may depend on how important the missing 5% is to the employer. If there are any gaps, you will need to come up with a very good argument as to how they will be bridged, if you want to be considered. We will cover some strategies to help you with this later in Part 7.

Should you find that the role isn't quite what you expected or you don't match what they are looking for, it may be that this role isn't for you – or at least not yet. It could be part of a longer-term strategy that you can work towards.

Salary research

Unless you are independently wealthy, it's important to know the market rates for the types of job you are interested in. There's lots of good salary information available online. Simply type into your internet search engine the keywords 'salary survey' along with your chosen job title or sector, and you will find a variety of different reports, for example 'salary survey supply chain jobs'.

However, before you get too carried away looking at the top end of the salary ranges, bear in mind that certain sectors tend to pay more than others and if employers are spoilt for choice they have less incentive to pay premium rates.

> ## TIP
>
> It's important to know the likely salary range for a job before you apply for it. If it's not listed, ring up the recruiter and ask. They'll usually tell you as there is no point in wasting either your or their time if it's not suitable.

Recruiters will want to know your current salary to determine your level of seniority. If there is too big a jump between what you have been earning and the salary in the new role, they may simply consider that you are too junior.

Talk to people

Inside information from people who are currently in the role or who hire for the role is invaluable. Seek out anyone who can give you the answers to the following questions and write their answers down.

- What does a typical day in this type of role involve?
- What are employers looking for when they recruit for this role?
- What differentiates the people who are good at this job?
- Do you think I'm suitable?
- What is the future demand for these types of role?
- What advice can you give me in applying for these roles?
- Will you let me know if you hear of suitable opportunities?

Work tasters

See if you can spend some time with someone who currently works in the role you are interested in. This might be a work placement, a voluntary assignment or even an unrelated temporary job in the department where you want to work. You will get an insight into the day-to-day reality of the job. You can also add it as relevant experience on your CV and use it as an opportunity to network and get advice while you are there.

Identify projects that can help you get a feel for a new line of work or style of working. Try to do these as extracurricular activities or parallel paths so that you can experiment seriously without making a commitment.

Hermina Ibarra, **Working Identity: Unconventional Strategies for Reinventing Your Career**

TIP

Use your existing contacts but also be proactive and go and talk directly to those who have the information you need. You can also use online forums such as LinkedIn to connect with people for advice.

Once you have completed as much research as you can, gather together the findings of your research below.

TIP

Be prepared for the research in this chapter to take you several hours, weeks or even months. It will be worth it as diligent research now will save you plenty of time downstream.

JOB RESEARCH SUMMARY

1. Answer the following questions for every role you have been considering. You may need to continue on another piece of paper.

What is a typical job title for this type of role?

What have you found out about the role?

How well does the role match your current skills and experience?

Are there any gaps between what you have to offer and what recruiters want? If so, how can you make up the gap?

What is the salary range?

How do people normally get into this role?

What are the advantages of this as a career choice for you?

Are there any disadvantages?

Does it take you closer to achieving your career visualisation? If so, how?

Is it a good fit for you as a career choice? If so, why?

EXAMPLE

What is a typical job title for this kind of role?
Online marketing assistant.

What have you found out about the role?
That it involves a mixture of technical and creative skills. Lots of time spent in front of the computer so very static. Very results driven. It needs lots of energy, writing skills and coming up with new ideas. It is very analytical as you need to keep a close eye on statistics and fine-tune what you are doing. Also about relationship building and brand building.

How well does the role match your current skills and experience?
My marketing degree will stand me in good stead. I understand the psychology of talking to customers. My strong visual creativity will also help in creating aesthetically pleasing and eye-catching content. I have very good IT skills.

Are there gaps between what you have to offer and what recruiters want? If so, how can you make up the gap?
Experience in search engine optimisation (SEO) and social media, which I have little experience of. I can read up all about SEO and using social media for business. I can also offer to help my current employer with their SEO, getting them listed in free directories, investigating pay per click campaigns. I can also talk to a couple of my friends who work in this area to find out more about what is involved.

What is the salary range?

Between £15k and £25k for first or second job in this area.

How do people normally get into this role?

Trainee role. Usually an IT/marketing background. Or they already work in the organisation and they take over responsibility for this as one of their duties.

What are the advantages of this as a career choice for you?

Great use of my marketing degree and IT skills. If I can find a role in which I can also use my creativity, e.g. sports or visual arts, then this would be ideal.

Are there any disadvantages?

No. Only that I am going to have to work hard to show that I am capable. May need to take a pay cut to get in at entry level but it will be worth it.

Does it take you closer to achieving your career picture?
If so, how?

I think the combination of IT and creativity will give me the job satisfaction I really want – and that was the biggest factor in my picture – my feeling that I could express myself at work.

Is it a good fit for you as a career choice? If so, why?

Yes, it is a really good use of my degree and uses a lot of my skills. I am sure that I could do well in this role.

Louis

EXERCISE 35 (CONT.)

2. Once you have done this, are your choices about your next career move becoming clearer? Is there one option that has become a clear favourite or are there two or three which still appeal?

3. Write down below the job option(s) that you would like to take forward to the next stage.

My preferred option(s)

1.

2.

3.

17 MAKING A DECISION

> *You've got a lot of choices. If getting out of bed in the morning is a chore and you're not smiling on a regular basis, try another choice.*
>
> **Steven D. Woodhull**

Now you've got your options, this chapter is about helping you make your decisions. We are going to use the research you've collected about you and your job choices to make sure that your next move is one that will give you what you are looking for career-wise.

Let's put some of your career ideas through their paces to find out whether they are realistic and robust.

Seven tips for effective career decision-making

1. Do your research

Gather together all the information and facts you need to help you make that decision. These may include written materials, opinions, statistics, advertisements and internet research. You should have lots of this from Chapters 15 and 16.

2. Listen to your intuition

If the facts say one thing but your gut instinct is telling you another, the mismatch is trying to tell you something. Work out what it is and whether it is valid or not.

3. Enjoy making decisions

Treat your career decision-making as an enjoyable research project. If you feel under pressure or are impatient to make a quick decision, slow down, or you could miss some important information that may hold you back later on.

4. Talk out loud

Many people find that talking through their options or decision with someone else is very helpful. So if you need to, find someone who is a good listener to bounce ideas off.

5. Don't catastrophise

There are very few things in life that are irreversible. Build in a review period once the decision has been made, and if you've given it all you've got and it's not working, try something else.

6. Manage risk

Every decision – including the decision to do nothing – has an element of risk. Accept that even with the best information in the world, you can't possibly know everything, cover every eventuality or guarantee success. However, if your career decision entails considerable financial risk, make sure you have a fall-back plan just in case.

7. Commit to your decision

Once you have made your decision, put all your energy behind it in order to make it work. The right decision executed half-heartedly is more likely to fail than the wrong decision implemented with gusto.

Considering your options

You may remember that right at the beginning of the coaching process we looked at the pros and cons of your current career situation (page 2). We are now going to do the same for your career options to make sure that you are taking as objective a view as you can.

PROS AND CONS

1. Write down below, or on a separate piece of paper, the advantages and disadvantages of each option you are considering.

2. Make notes, including any implications, queries or conditions that may apply.

Pros	Cons	Notes

EXAMPLE

Becoming a physics teacher

Pros	Cons	Notes
Like working with kids	Need for substantial retraining	
Works around family life better than current job	May still need to arrange childcare depending on location of school	Can probably come to an arrangement
Could work more locally	No guarantee would find a local job	
Personal interest in the subject	Not all the kids may be interested	
Fits with my values of making a difference	Would I find the organisation a bit slow compared with the fast pace of where I've been?	
More scope for creativity than in my current job	Lots of bureaucracy to deal with which I may find frustrating	Friend who is a teacher has been telling me about all the paperwork
Regular income	Drop in salary	

Raj

It may be that at this stage one option is coming out as a clear favourite. However, if there are a few that still seem equally attractive, the next exercise will help you weigh up the options in more detail.

DECISION-MAKING WORKSHEET

If there are a number of options you are considering, try the following comparison worksheet to help you choose. The example on page 160 shows you how it works.

1. Think of your career wish list and career picture (Exercises 30 and 31). List up to 10 of your career priorities for the future and rank them in terms of their importance to you, making the most important priority number 10 and the least important number 1.

2. Insert the options you are considering, for example staying where you are, starting your own business, moving to a similar job in a new company.

3. In the Probability column, decide how likely it is that this option will satisfy the priorities that are important to you: 10 means that it is very probable and 1 is unlikely. Your market research will be useful here.

4. Multiply the Career Priorities Ranking number by the Probability number and enter it into the subtotal for that column for that option. Then add the subtotal scores up for each option at the bottom of the column to show how each option compares in respect of meeting your career requirements.

TIP

Feel free to adjust the priorities and weighting if needed and play around with different options. See page 160 for an example.

DECISION-MAKING WORKSHEET

Career priorities	Career priorities ranking (1–10)	Option 1		Option 2		Option 3	
		Probability	Subtotal	Probability	Subtotal	Probability	Subtotal
Total							

EXAMPLE

Career priorities	Career priorities ranking (1–10)	Option 1 Move to similar job in new organisation		Option 2 Stay where I am		Option 3 Retrain as a teacher	
		Probability	Subtotal	Probability	Subtotal	Probability	Subtotal
More money	10	5	50	1	10	1	10
Promotion opportunities	9	4	36	1	9	1	9
Recognition for my work	8	5	40	1	8	2	16
Security	7	1	7	5	35	6	42
More responsibility	6	5	30	1	6	4	24
Work in a sector that is growing not contracting	5	6	30	1	5	5	25
Good journey into work	4	7	28	7	28	9	36
Offers leadership training and development	3	4	12	2	6	5	15
To feel at end of day that I have made a difference	2	5	10	1	2	8	16
To have good bunch of people to work with	1	4	4	4	4	5	5
Total			247		113		198

You can see from the example that moving into a similar role in a new organisation emerges as the preferred option in this instance.

If you are at all uncertain that the option which emerged from Exercise 37 is the right one for you, double-check by completing the following decision-making exercise.

Final check

Very often when we make decisions, we use a preferred decision-making style. We may choose an analytical approach or tend to rely on 'gut feelings'. Optimists may underestimate difficulties or assume they don't need a contingency plan because everything is just going to work out fine. On the other hand, pessimists can get so wrapped up in the pitfalls they miss the boat.

> *Both optimists and pessimists contribute to our society. The optimist invents the airplane and the pessimist the parachute.*
> **Gil Stern**

The following exercise forces you to move outside your normal thinking and decision-making style to obtain a more balanced view.

EXERCISE 38

DECISION PERSPECTIVES

Take your preferred option and test it thoroughly from all perspectives. Answer all questions below, and write down your answers.

Facts
Do you have all the information you need?

What factual evidence do you have that this option is realistic?

Have other people confirmed that this option is realistic?

Emotions
What emotion(s) do you feel when thinking about this option?

What does this reaction tell you about the option you have chosen?

How do you think others will react emotionally to this career decision?

Negatives
What are the downsides to this option?

Why might it not work?

What would happen if this option didn't work out?

Positives
What appeals to you about this option?

What could it mean for you if you succeed?

How might others benefit if you succeed?

Creativity
If you had complete freedom, what would you do?

Did you generate lots of different ideas before making your decision?

Are there any other routes you could take?

Systems
What processes need to be in place for this option to work?

How will you know if this option is working or not?

Who and what will keep you on track?

EXAMPLE

Facts

I have looked at my finances and all the study options and decided to do a distance-learning course because I can work at the same time. I will ask work to support me because I can argue that it is in line with my job, but I'm prepared to fund it myself if they don't. I have spoken with recruiters and they have told me that it would definitely be an advantage to me if I had this qualification. I have also spoken to two people who work in this field who have told me the same.

Emotions

I feel apprehensive about investing this money and the fact that it is going to be tough to find the time in the evenings and at weekends to do the work. However, I feel very focused that this is the right thing to do. I feel relieved that the qualification will give me more credibility whereas in the past sometimes I felt like I have been winging it. My partner will be very supportive but might get a bit fed up that a lot of my free time will be taken up with the course.

Negatives

My time is going to be in very short supply, stretched between work, studying and home life. I might fail the course or not complete it.

However, as the course is flexible learning, I can always take a break between modules if it's all getting too much. The worst thing would be if I spent all this time and energy on the course and then stayed where I was in my job. Must make sure that doesn't happen.

Positives

Am genuinely interested in the subject. I am looking forward to becoming qualified. I like the fact that this is something I have wanted to do for ages. If I succeed in moving into a new job in this area then I will feel very happy. It fits with what I want from my career; my job satisfaction I think will greatly increase as well as my opportunities to progress further. I think also people will be really proud of me.

Creativity

I would definitely still want to do the course but I would start applying for jobs now rather than waiting to finish studying. I wonder if I could apply for jobs telling them that I am about to start studying? There is nothing to stop me joining the networking groups at the institute and LinkedIn to start making connections. I could also talk to those guys I met at the exhibition. The other route I could take is to move to an organisation that specialises in this area and make an internal move.

Systems

My time management needs to improve as I'm going to be juggling work, home and study and looking for a new job. Probably need to allocate set days to do homework. Also will need to make special time for partner to keep relationship sweet. Perhaps I should plan out my diary in advance. Because the course is in complete modules, I can review at the end of each module how it is going, take a breather and then plan for the next one. Alongside studying I will need to keep an eye on any suitable job opportunities – don't want to miss anything because I'm too busy.

Phil

CAREER DECISION-MAKING CHECKLIST

Let's make sure you can tick off all of the following items in your decision-making checklist.

You have ...	Yes
Considered different options before making your decision	☐
Researched exactly what the role involves	☐
Talked to people who work in the field	☐
Looked at job adverts for similar roles	☐
Identified any gaps and how to fill them	☐
Checked likely salary levels	☐
Talked to recruiters/employers who hire for these roles	☐
Considered any personal factors that might have an impact	☐
Weighed up both the advantages and disadvantages of this option	☐

MY CAREER DECISION: WHAT IS MY GOAL?

We have looked at your options, researched and then evaluated them to help you decide on your next career move and your career objectives.

We have also rigorously tested your preferred option to make sure that, as far as we can tell, it is realistic and workable for you.

Some options you have considered will be immediate goals, while some may be longer term. These are important to bear in mind and will be incorporated into the Career Action Plan we will be developing together in Part 9.

If you are clear on your decision, write it down. Include both your immediate and longer-term goals.

I decide to:

EXAMPLE

I decide to:

- *start my course even if I have to fund it myself*
- *use the course to increase my employability in this field*
- *make time for my partner while I am studying*
- *increase my specialisation in this field so I become an industry expert*
- *look for a new job in this sector.*

Phil

This exercise will help you fill out your career goals in exercise 44 on page 276 and you will be revisiting it when you compile your Career Action Plan in Part 9.

EXERCISE 41

REFLECTING ON PART 5

Review the following exercises:

- Exercise 30: Career wish list (page 116)
- Exercise 31: Visualising the future (page 118)
- Exercise 32: Interesting options (page 134)
- Exercise 33: Your ideas (page 140)
- Exercise 34: Interpreting job ads (page 145)
- Exercise 35: Job research summary (page 150)
- Exercise 36: Pros and cons (page156)

- Exercise 37: Decision-making worksheet (page 158)
- Exercise 38: Decision perspectives (page 161)
- Exercise 39: Career decision-making checklist (page 165)
- Exercise 40: My career decision: what is my goal? (page 165)

Let's take a few moments to capture any other thoughts, ideas or information that have surfaced. These might include the following.

- What has been helpful to you in this section?
- Were you surprised at your decision or is it what you expected?
- What emotions have you felt while working on this section and why?
- Any other comments.
- Any actions you want to take.

My reflections on my options and decisions

Action points

EXAMPLE

I felt frustrated that I couldn't step right into the job I wanted. Recruiters simply did not feel that I had the experience needed and that I was wasting my time applying. This was a bit of a blow but at least it explains why I'm not getting shortlisted.

I am going to have to approach it in steps rather than making the big leap I hoped. A couple of people told me that they thought I should try to get into the right type of organisation and try to achieve a sideways move from within. This is how they did it, so I am going to try this. However, my research came up with a couple of other suggestions that are also interesting and perhaps easier for me to achieve, so I am going to look at both options in tandem.

Action points

1. *Identify the roles I could apply for that would give me a way into the organisations I want to work for.*

2. *Find out from my contacts which organisations tend to be more flexible in how they deploy their staff.*

3. *Continue researching some of my other career ideas.*

Aseem

We will revisit this reflections exercise when we look back on your career coaching journey in Part 9.

In Part 5 we explored your options and hopefully you are now clearer about what you want for the future.

If you are still unclear, then it's worth revisiting your research and talking it through with someone who can help you make sense of it. Alternatively you may just hit a career block and, if so, the next section will provide some strategies to help.

PART 6

Blocks and bridges

Now that you are clear about where you are heading career-wise, let's anticipate some of the blocks you might encounter on your journey and what you can do to counter them. This section will also help you identify the people who can act as a bridge to your new career situation.

In this section we will:

- identify your career blocks

- suggest strategies to help you overcome those blocks

- draw up a list of people who can help you

18 WHAT MIGHT GET IN THE WAY?

Let's face it: if it was easy for people to make the changes in their career that would make them happy, the job satisfaction ratings for employees in the UK wouldn't be so low.

> A 2016 CIPD/Halogen survey finds that almost a 23% of employees believe their organisation's performance management processes are unfair, 27% are dissatisfied with the opportunity to develop their skills in their job and 36% say they are unlikely to fulfil their career aspirations in their current organisation.

So let's also take a moment to anticipate some of the challenges you might face along the way.

There are some common problems that people face when trying to make changes in their career or working life. These 'career blocks' tend to fall into two categories.

1. **External blocks.** These are practical and tangible impediments. An example might be a gap in your qualifications or limited work experience for the type of job you want. It could also include real personal constraints such as your availability to work, or family commitments that restrict your ability to travel.

2. **Internal blocks.** These are more psychological in nature but they can be powerful enough to scupper even the best laid career plans. They may be rooted in issues like poor self-esteem, discomfort with risk or feelings of hopelessness. These blocks may have developed relatively recently or have been something that have been around for a long time, even since childhood.

Common career blocks

This isn't an exhaustive list, but here are some common career blocks that can surface.

External blocks	Internal blocks
Lack of information	Lack of focus
Financial needs	Low self-esteem
Skills/experience gaps	Over-confidence
Training/qualification	Fear of rejection/failure
Family needs	Too modest
Strong competition	Pessimism/hopelessness
Insufficient time	Too idealistic
Discrimination	Anxiety
Location	Too tolerant
Lack of support	Dislike of change/uncertainty
Few connections	Fear of disappointing others
Health needs	Indecisiveness
Sector changes	Too spontaneous
Scarcity of jobs sought	Low trust of others
Recruiter perceptions	Disorganised

Individuals tend to be very alert to the **external** career blocks they are facing, but less attuned to the effect their **internal** blocks can have on their career progress. In many cases, external blocks can be overcome with determination, lateral thinking and by finding some compromise which will make your career goal more realistic. However, the most robust, well-researched career action plan may fail to get off the ground if you are struggling with negative self-talk, poor confidence or some self-defeating behaviours.

Let's look at some of those career blocks and some strategies which may help.

Tackling common career blocks
I'm worried that if I try, I will fail and look stupid

Most people will have some understanding of this block. No one likes to fail or look stupid. In itself this isn't a problem – in fact it's a great incentive to do everything you can to succeed. However, if 'the fear of failure' is the big black cloud that is keeping you stuck where you are, then let's look at your worst fear head on, to see whether in fact failure deserves its negative reputation.

Are there actually any advantages to having tried and failed? Without the experience of failure, you would not be able to:

- learn from your mistakes – know how to do it better next time
- understand where the gaps are
- reality-check your expectations
- know what contingency plan you need next time
- ask others for help and advice on what you now know are the problem areas
- avoid regrets for missed opportunities.

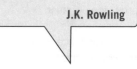

I was the biggest failure I knew … It is impossible to live without failing at something, unless you live so cautiously that you might as well not have lived at all – in which case, you fail by default.

J.K. Rowling

Who would have thought?

- Jamie Oliver – left school with two GCSEs
- Richard Branson – poor academic record due to dyslexia
- Simon Cowell – bankrupt at 30 and living with his parents
- Bill Gates – university drop-out
- Michael Jordan – dropped from high school basketball team for 'lack of skill'
- Steven Spielberg – rejected three times by University of Southern California film school.

In most cases, people's fear of failure is disproportionate to the actual effect a real failure would have. If you were unsuccessful in applying for a promotion or a new job, what would happen? Not a lot – you continue as before. If you made a job move but it didn't work out, what would you do? Get yourself another job as soon as you could and move on.

You should also avoid the assumption that staying where you are is always a safer option. This is not always the case. If there are threats to your job or you are under stress, it could be far riskier to do nothing, both to your job prospects and your health. If you think that this might be an issue for you, go back to page 124, where we discuss the pros and cons of doing nothing about your job situation.

I would love to, but I don't have the confidence

Whether you want to ask your boss for career development, or impress a potential new employer at interview, appearing to have confidence in your own abilities is a prerequisite for other people taking you seriously.

> *If you think you can do a thing or think you can't do a thing, you're right.*
>
> **Henry Ford**

There are very few people who would say privately that they are entirely free of self-doubts. I coach many highly successful people who would appear to the outside world to be brimming over with confidence, but who, like most other people, frequently question whether they are 'good enough'.

In this respect, it is not the fact that you have self-doubts that is important. We all have them – it's just part of human nature. What matters is whether you let them hold you back.

I remember working with a highly capable senior manager who had been made redundant along with many of her colleagues. She was someone who had very low self-esteem, but in her organisation she was very highly thought of and had been continuously promoted. She ascribed her rise through the ranks to being 'so worried they were going to find out that I was rubbish that I worked harder than anyone else to keep them from finding out'.

Facing redundancy could have been her worst nightmare come true, given her usual state of anxiety. However, within a week she had two good job offers. 'I was so scared that I was never going to work again that I went absolutely hell for leather to find a new job. I didn't waste a moment – ringing everyone, getting my CV sorted, pulling in favours, networking like mad. I'm lucky it worked!'

> *Even if you are on the right track you'll get run over if you just sit there.*
>
> **Will Rogers**

Of course, it wasn't luck. She is a classic example of someone who has very little personal confidence but who was able to use her fear and pessimism constructively as a motivator to take action.

However, there are lots of other circumstances where people do let their lack of confidence get in the way. Either because they are too modest to talk about their achievements, reluctant to put themselves forward because they fear rejection or failure and a tendency to be passive rather than proactive in their career so that they miss out on opportunities. Here are some tips if you feel that your confidence could do with a boost.

Building your self-confidence

1. Think of your past successes. Review Part 3 to remind yourself of past achievements, your skills and abilities. Write down all the nice things that people have said about you.

2. Spend time with positive people who are supportive, encouraging and have your best interests at heart. Avoid whingers who just want you to moan with them.

3. Remember your picture of your ideal working day (Exercise 31, page 118). Create the picture in your head as vividly as you can. Revert back to this picture regularly to keep you on track.

4. Exercise and eat healthily. Exercise increases those feel-good endorphins and clears the mind. Yoga, meditation or even just going for a walk can help you work off nervous energy and reduce anxiety.

5. Refresh your image. A new haircut and outfit that is smart and contemporary can give a real boost to your confidence.

6. Experiment with new ideas or approaches in a safe environment. For instance, if you want to practise your networking skills, start with family and friends, graduating to other people you know and then to complete strangers.

I know from my coaching clients that sometimes what is needed is more than just a confidence boost. A tricky career situation can trigger powerful feelings. For instance it's common for individuals experiencing redundancy to feel varying degrees of anger, resentment and a sense of betrayal. When this is combined with perhaps some longer term self-esteem issues and anxiety about the future, it can turn into a potent psychological brew. Statistics tell us that one in four people at any one time are contending with a mental health challenge and whether this was caused by work issues or not, there is no doubt that an individual's sense of well-being will impact on how well they are able to handle a difficult workplace or career situation.

So if you do find that you are feeling anxious, not sleeping well, have a pervading sense of hopelessness or anger then it's important that first and foremost you look after yourself. This might be about following some of the self-help suggestions above but it's also worth talking to your doctor or a counsellor because any input that can help you counter emotional stress and negative self-talk will help you both personally and professionally.

I'd love to make a career move but I just can't afford to

This career block can take a number of forms, including:

- expecting that the career move will mean a drop in salary
- worrying about the financial risks of changing the status quo
- not being able to afford the training required for the new role
- waiting for a bonus or redundancy payment before moving
- not having the financial resources to set up on your own
- believing job satisfaction is a luxury and unrealistic.

If you are worried about the financial implications of taking a new role, it is very important that your concerns are built on accurate information rather than perception. Sit down and look at your personal finances to establish your financial needs and any flexibility you might have. Take some financial advice if necessary. We often spend according to our budget rather than our needs, so be clear about what your salary essentials are, rather than basing your assumptions on your current salary. Also, bear in mind the longer term: could there be greater earning potential for the future with this new role? Are there other benefits, such as a pension scheme, or could it perhaps mean a quicker, cheaper journey for you into work?

Is there a stepping-stone role you could take in the right direction, which would be close enough to your current position to attract a similar salary package? This is often a very workable solution. For instance, I remember working with a lawyer who was desperate to leave the legal profession and go into business, but who was worried about a drop in salary. He moved to a business consultancy role where his legal background was a huge asset because the organisation's principal customers were legal firms.

If the new role requires you to undertake costly training or a vocational course, investigate whether there are other less expensive routes, perhaps a shorter course or on-the-job training. Could you do the training as part of an evening course so that you can continue to bring in an income during the day? Can you get a student loan to help you pay for the course?

In the event that your job is under threat from redundancy, check out the size of any potential redundancy payment. It may be less than you think, especially if you are only entitled to statutory redundancy monies. In which case it may be better for you to move into a new job as soon as you can, rather than risk a gap in employment when your job ends.

> ## TIP
>
> Check out www.acas.org.uk for details of your statutory redundancy entitlements.

And if you would love to set up your own business, the only way you are going to know if you can afford to is to devise a proper business plan so you know exactly what your commitments and risks would be. On pages 247–250 there is more information for anyone who is considering self-employment.

You can see from the above that there are lots of things you can do to overcome a 'block' connected with financial feasibility. However, it's worth noting that individuals often identify a 'finances' block as an external block when a little more investigation shows that it has more to do with internal factors, like a lack of commitment to the goal or a fear of failure.

TIP

Make sure you have done your calculations thoroughly and counted the opportunity costs of staying where you are before deciding whether a job move is financially feasible for you or not.

I just don't have the time to focus on my career – I'm too busy doing my job

If you are currently working, it's understandable that at the end of a hard day you may just want to relax. You might also have the dinner to make, the kids' homework to help with, or the gym to visit. In fact there are a million and one other things that you could be doing rather than investing time in making your career work. But, like anything else in life, you get out what you put in, and if you want something enough **you make the time!**

Smart time management is especially critical if you are currently working in a role that is demanding. You must continue to do a good job for your employer, while freeing yourself up some time to work on furthering your career plan.

Below are some ideas which can make your time management more effective and reduce the potency of that age-old excuse, 'I haven't got time'.

- Make a time schedule. Set yourself tasks and target dates for completion – and stick to them.
- Allocate specific times to work on your career, for example set aside Monday evenings to research, send off emails and work on your CV.
- Delegate what you can and decide what can wait. The house may need cleaning but in the same time you could have sent off several job applications. Defer routine tasks or shorten them, but don't use them as an excuse.

- Use your lunch breaks effectively, to meet with people, or ring up prospective employers.
- Stop staying late at work – leave work on time. Don't send or respond to emails at weekends or in the evenings unless they are urgent.
- Generate opportunities at work which will be developmental for you and beneficial to the company, such as spending time building relationships with customers and suppliers who could in the future become your new employer.
- Volunteer to help out at exhibitions and conferences where you can get to meet other people in your industry.

TIP

The Career Action Plan we'll complete in Part 9 will help you devise a schedule with tasks and target dates for completion.

At a time when people are working longer and harder than ever before, it can be tricky to find the time you need. However, you can always find the time if you are motivated to do so.

If you find yourself saying 'Yes, but …', be honest. It's not the time management that is constraining you; it's something else. Work out what it really is – you can then start tackling the real issue not the pretend one.

I don't have the information I need

We live in a time when our access to information is unrivalled. The internet is a vast information resource and you have only to type keywords into your computer or even your phone to find out about career opportunities, specific jobs, training courses, job-hunting strategies and market trends.

There are many ways to access information, outlined in Chapter 16 – go back and make sure you have researched these fully. It will take time and effort to carry out the research you need, so expect it to require hard work. You may also need to accept that even with the best information in the world, you can't possibly know everything. You may just need to take a view and make your best guess.

It may be that your concerns are not about a lack of information at all, but relate more to an internal career block such as risk aversion. Consider what is going on for you emotionally as the difficulty may lie here.

I know what I want to do, but I don't have the skills, qualifications or experience I need to compete with others already working in this area

First, make sure you investigate exactly what you need, rather than making assumptions. Look again at Chapter 16 to ensure that you have done all the research and reality-checking necessary to come to that conclusion. You could also do the following.

- Find the post-holders of jobs you are interested in on LinkedIn and look through their previous career history to see how they got there.
- Ask people who currently work in the field whether they know of anyone who came into the post from an alternative route.
- If you need a particular qualification for the role, make arrangements to start studying for it and say on your CV that this is what you are doing. This will show your commitment to your chosen career path and help reassure any potential employer that you will be able to bridge an important shortfall.
- If you can persuade your current employer that the skills and qualification would be of benefit in your current job, they may be willing to sponsor your training.
- Arrange to shadow someone. This could be a formal arrangement through work or an informal arrangement that you have organised yourself. Either way, it gives you relevant content to talk about on your CV and at interview.
- Consider voluntary work to plug some of the gaps. Being a member of the PTA or a governor at a school, joining a charity committee or organising a fundraising event can offer opportunities for you to extend your people management skills and project management abilities, and deepen your understanding of budget management, strategy development and organisational communications.

> *I wanted to move from a technical role to a managerial one but had no experience of managing staff or strategy. I joined a management committee of a local training college and got involved in all kinds of issues from recruitment to devising strategy, governance and financial issues. It was fantastic learning. My company were so impressed that I had done this on my own initiative that they put me on the fast-track promotion panel for a managerial career. They loved my initiative and thought that that in itself was sufficient evidence of my management capabilities.*
>
> **Rory**

If you have truly investigated all of the above and it is still evident that you don't stand a chance, you can:

- consider a stepping-stone role that may be similar to what you are already doing, but enables you to work in an organisation or sector that is more relevant to your target role. From there you can plot your next move to get even closer
- accept that the role is beyond your reach and focus on one that is more achievable.

I've family responsibilities and I'm not sure that I can put my career first

If your current role complements your home life, enabling you to pay the bills, offering security, convenience and a reasonable work/life balance, then you may decide that while your current job isn't perfect, you are better off staying where you are. And you might be right.

However, there could still be other opportunities out there that might be even better. If you don't even look, then how are you to know?

For instance, going for a promotion does not automatically mean that you will have less family time. Often, the more senior you are, the more freedom you have to schedule your own diary. It can be easier to take the time off to attend the school play if you are a manager than if you are an assistant.

There is never any harm in looking around for jobs, networking, trying to create opportunities. Even if you get offered a job, you don't have to accept it if you don't feel it is right for you. But unless you start looking you will never know whether there is a role that might suit your current family circumstances better than your existing situation.

I feel I am being treated unfairly at work

If you are in an uncomfortable situation at work, it is essential that you start trying to do something about it.

I remember talking to a guy who worked for a manager who was an absolute bully. He was making his life hell. However, he said that he felt he couldn't move because he needed the regular money his role brought in.

What he didn't seem to have factored in is that no one – least of all his family – wanted him to stay in that situation. He was highly employable. What had happened was that his confidence had gone, he was highly stressed and he had lost faith in himself and his ability to go and find another job – so he wasn't even trying. His plan was to keep his head low, grit his teeth and bear it. What a grim prospect for anyone – knowing that the longer he stayed there, the lower his confidence would sink.

TIP

If you feel you are being harassed or bullied at work, contact either www.gov.uk/workplace-bullying-and-harassment or www.mind.org.uk.

My age is against me – that is why I am not getting shortlisted

Discrimination exists. It is often subtle and hard to prove, but there are undoubtedly some cases where individuals are rejected because of some prejudice of the recruiter.

At a seminar I ran recently, I asked 'Who feels their age is against them in looking for a new job?' Every single person in the room put their hand up, from the 18-year-old through to the 65-year-old. In fact most clients I have ever worked with have expressed the fear that they thought their age was against them. However, in my experience, many people who feel they have been discriminated against – whether on the grounds of age, sex, race or disability – have actually been rejected because of other concerns with their CV or career history.

I recently spoke with a 30-year-old woman who felt that she wasn't getting interviews because employers probably thought that she was going to go off and have babies. Well, possibly – but when I looked at her CV, it was far more likely to be the spelling mistakes that were putting off prospective employers than her age.

With regard to age, it is, of course, true that some industries are more youth-orientated than others. Organisations specialising in social media and web design, for instance, tend to have younger staff. Clearly if you walk into an organisation where most of the people are considerably younger than you, it's going to be harder to make it look as though you fit in. However, on the whole, people will hire you for the contribution you can make to their organisation. Show them how you can add value and your age becomes irrelevant.

If you are not landing jobs for which you know you are suitable, then you need to a take a hard look at your applications and get some honest feedback. Is it your age? Or have you really shown that you can deliver what the employer is looking for?

Make sure your applications are as good as they can be and that you address head-on any potentially discriminatory misconceptions by the employer. For instance if you are a more mature worker, ensure that your CV comes over as high-energy, that you show how up-to-date you are, that you have learned new skills, and that you have recent achievements. This is the best way to address discrimination – by making the best darn application you can.

Bear in mind that the abolition of the compulsory retirement age and demographics means that more and more people will be working longer, so a more mature workforce is going to be the norm.

> ## TIP
>
> See pages 262–263 for advice if you are worried about being an older worker in the job market

I don't have any networking connections

Unless you stay in a sealed room for most of your day, you are bound to know people with whom you can network.

> *I happened to talk to a fellow dog walker and started talking about work. She told me her husband had just started work at the local business park and they were recruiting a lot of people. I sent my application in and that's how I got my job.*
>
> **Harriet**

Your first port of call is family and friends. They are your warmest personal contacts, yet probably the most underused in networking terms. Whether you're a graduate or a more mature job-seeker you should be asking all your family members and friends for any introductions and advice on getting your next job. You don't know who your family and friends know until you ask. (See Chapter 20 for more advice on how family and friends can help your career.) Beyond that, remember that anyone you meet in whatever circumstance could be a helpful contact. A client told me that he was catching a train recently and started talking to someone he recognised as one of the dads involved in running his son's football team. Their conversation turned to work and he offered to forward his CV to the relevant manager. The guy clearly put in a good word for him, he got a meeting and was subsequently hired.

> ## TIP
>
> Exercise 43 (page 192) will help you draw up your contact list.

Actively go out and network with people. Go to conferences, professional associations and community events to talk to people there.

Lastly, social media has developed all kinds of ways that people can come together to chat online. Join LinkedIn to build your online business profile and connect with those you know as well as new contacts through joining relevant interest groups. Facebook is a way of keeping in touch easily with family and friends and asking informally for advice and information.

TIP

If you are on Facebook, make sure that you keep your business and personal life separate.

I'm worried that my career to date will be viewed negatively

It may be that you have had a number of shorter-term jobs, a career break, a period of unemployment, or that you left your last job in unhappy circumstances. Most people, if you ask them about their career, will have had some bumpier times.

There are two things to remember. First, downplay whatever the issue is rather than drawing attention to it. For instance, using a functional CV that lists all your relevant skills and experiences on the front page and relegates your employment dates to the second page can reduce the visibility of any career irregularities that would be very noticeable on a chronological CV.

Second, prospective employers will be largely influenced by how you talk about those problems, rather than the problem itself. Avoid the temptation to justify yourself by blaming others. Candidates who criticise past employers and blame them for their woes are very unattractive to an employer, no matter how true their claims are.

If you have been made redundant, as many people have at some point in their careers, talk about it as a tough business decision that the organisation made about your department, rather than a personal tragedy for you. If you didn't stay very long in one job, rather than talking negatively about how awful it was, find a positive rationale for leaving – such as a new opportunity that was simply too good to miss.

Most people's careers have ups and downs. Take it in your stride – focus on the positives and the employer is likely to view it positively too.

> ## TIP
>
> See pages 252–255 for advice on dealing with any career skeletons when you are job-hunting.

It's such a competitive job market – there's no way I'm going to stand out

It's always competitive as the job you want other people will want too. It may therefore seem surprising that many employers complain that when it comes to candidates, they don't feel spoilt for choice. This is not due to a shortage of people able to do the job, but because most candidates do not market themselves as persuasively as they might. This includes submitting a CV with errors, interviewing badly, or failing to understand the employers' requirements. Part 7 of this book gives you lots of advice on how to perfect your sales pitch, to help you stand out from the crowd but, wherever you can, get some advice and feedback from career professionals or recruiters to maximise your chances of being shortlisted.

EXERCISE 42

WHAT ARE YOUR CAREER BLOCKS?

Now let's identify what, if any, career blocks you might have.

What blocks or difficulties, do you think could get in the way of achieving your goals? (External and internal.)

Have you encountered these in the past? If so, what helped you overcome them then?

What can you do to anticipate and overcome your career blocks?

EXAMPLE

What blocks or other difficulties, do you think could get in the way of achieving your goals? (External and internal.)

Although I've worked mainly in contract/temp roles I've really wanted to get a permanent role but as soon as recruiters see how many jobs I've had they only seem to put me up for temp roles. I have to earn money so whenever the agency has suggested a role I've accepted it even if I wasn't that keen, because I've been worried that nothing else would come along. But then I go into the role demoralised from the start because I feel that this is all I can get and I don't really want to be there. This then makes my CV look even worse and even less likely I will get a permanent job.

Have you encountered these in the past? If so, what helped you overcome them then?

It's always been difficult to persuade recruiters to consider me for permanent jobs. I do feel very pessimistic that this will change and as I get older I think this will be even more of a problem and even more frustrating. However, I do remember one assignment which I refused because the pay was just too low and I was glad that I did because a much better assignment came along.

What can you do to anticipate and overcome your career blocks?

Perhaps I need to be clearer with the agencies because if they know I will always do an emergency temp job, there may not be an incentive for them to put me up for permanent roles. Maybe be more choosy about the jobs I do? And I do know I have to watch my frustrations don't spill out at work because I did lose one potentially good temp-to-permanent opportunity because they liked my work, they just didn't think I wanted to be there.

Ann

TIP

We will revisit this exercise when we create your Career Insights document on page 291.

19 GETTING A HELPING HAND

In Chapter 18 we looked at some of the common career blocks that surface when people are trying to progress their career. One of the most effective ways of bridging many of those difficulties is by asking for support from other people.

People often feel apprehensive about asking others for advice. However, if you ask nicely, are duly appreciative and mindful of their time, then most people are very happy to help. In fact it's one of the things that people like doing best – telling others how they should be doing it.

In this chapter we look at who can help and how. You will also develop your own contact list of people whose input will be useful in the pursuit of your career goals (Exercise 44 on page 276).

Your manager

Hopefully you have already been able to get feedback from your manager or an ex-manager using the 360-degree feedback exercise (Exercise 28, page 107). If you haven't, then arrange a career development discussion. A good time to have this is either at your regular performance review meetings, after a success at work or if you have applied or been rejected for an internal role. Here are some tips for managing that discussion.

Gather the information

Prepare well for this meeting by gathering together previous appraisal information, internal job listings, and information about jobs and courses that interest you. You may also want to do some external benchmarking by looking at external job adverts and talking to recruiters, etc, to see how you compare with your peers as well as those who are in the jobs you want to apply for next.

Manage your manager

At the meeting, emphasise that this discussion is about your career development within your current organisation so that you can improve your performance, develop your skills and potentially take on new responsibilities. This is something that your boss is likely to see a direct benefit from so they will be more inclined to support it. Some managers will be open to talking with you about external possibilities but tread carefully because if they think you are about to leave then they may not want to invest time and resources in you.

> ## TIP
>
> If you show your employer that you are proactive about your career, they are more likely to see you as promotion material.

Listen attentively

Some managers are more soft skilled than others, but if they feel you are listening with an open mind and are valuing what they are saying, they are more likely to be forthcoming and honest with their feedback and advice. This is not to say that you shouldn't challenge their comments if you believe they are wrong, but if you find yourself slipping into a defensive mode, then try to switch the discussion to a constructive, joint-problem-solving type of approach.

> ## TIP
>
> It's not the HR department's job to manage your career: it's yours! But they can be very helpful if you ask for their advice.

Focus on the positives

Avoid moaning about the lack of promotion prospects or complaining about colleagues or senior management. Ask for advice on what you can do in the face of current constraints rather than attacking any injustices. Even if it becomes clear that your future career lies elsewhere, don't make any implied or explicit threats to leave. It's far better to work on this discreetly in your own time, rather than accelerate an unplanned exit.

Generate ideas

Ask your manager for their ideas so this feels like a joint idea-generating exercise but also have some good ideas that you have researched and are ready to discuss, for example:

- job enrichment by taking on some new relevant duties
- work shadowing or a secondment
- spending time 'client-side' or with a key supplier
- joining a cross-organisational project group
- becoming an ambassador or external representative for the company
- initiating a research project
- coaching, mentoring or getting involved in recruitment or training
- training courses, e-learning, webinars, joining a professional institutes
- volunteer activities, for example organising an event or sitting on a charity management committee
- writing articles, blogs or content for the company website or social media pages.

Agree an action plan

Don't forget to get agreement from your manager about what practical steps will be taken arising from this meeting and a review date to check on progress. Put this in an email to them afterwards so you both have a record of what was agreed.

The HR department

If your organisation has an HR team, ask for a meeting with them to find out more about career development opportunities within the organisation. Let them know what you are interested in and they may well have some relevant suggestions, including roles that may be on the horizon but not advertised yet. This will give you an opportunity to go and talk to the hiring manager ahead of time to declare your interest and suitability.

Even if there are no suitable vacancies, your HR department may be able to suggest career development opportunities which could take you closer to achieving your career goals. Many big organisations have a fast-track talent pool. If you're not sure, find out if they have one and what you need to do to be considered. Other development opportunities could include:

- internal and external training courses
- secondment
- volunteering on a project group
- having a mentor or mentoring others
- e-learning programmes

- organising a corporate event
- inducting new recruits and training others
- involvement in employer-sponsored volunteering.

If your organisation doesn't have an HR team, this discussion is more likely to take place with your manager or perhaps another senior manager whose responsibilities encompass HR.

TIP

Remember that no matter who you are talking to about your career development, you should be asking them for advice but also going in prepared with some ideas of your own. If your ideas are low-cost, easy to arrange and you offer to make up any time that is lost, it is much more likely that your boss will agree to them.

Colleagues

If you work for a large organisation, try to build up a grapevine of contacts throughout the organisation. Go for lunch or a coffee with more distant colleagues to find out what is happening in their part of the organisation. It will give you a very different perspective and alert you to potential opportunities.

However, be a bit careful about how much you confide in colleagues, especially if your career goals are likely to impact on them or the organisation. Sometimes it is advisable to be discreet rather than too open.

Customers and suppliers

In the course of your work you come into contact with many external people. Think about all the people you interact with every day. Many an employee has jumped ship to work with an organisation that was originally their customer. If you have a good working relationship with an external company, they may see you, potentially, as a good member of staff for them. This situation needs to be handled carefully as you don't want to compromise your relationship with either the customer or your own organisation.

> When I lost my job I contacted the suppliers I had worked with. I had been a tough negotiator so I figured they would want me on their side next time. I was right!
>
> **Anita**

However, there is no harm in asking how they recruit their staff because you might be interested in applying to them in the future. If there is something suitable, they will probably tell you, but if not, you will have planted a seed which means that they may well come back to you at a later date.

> ## TIP
>
> If you do end up working for a company that has a relationship with your own, assure both companies that you will not be spilling any commercially sensitive information; stress that your aim is to use your knowledge of working on both sides to improve upon the relationship even further.

Professional forums

Volunteer for opportunities where you can represent the company externally and which will bring you into contact with other people and their organisations. This could include helping out at exhibition stands, going to conferences or reporting back from industry forums.

I got my last job as a result of a casual conversation over coffee with someone who turned out to be the finance director of a competitor.

Henry

One of the main purposes of these events is networking, sharing information, checking out the competition and discussing business challenges. Swap business cards where you can, follow up with an email – and use those connections when appropriate.

See pages 234–237 for more advice on professional networking.

Mentors

A mentor is normally someone in your field who has a more senior background than you, and who is happy to give you the benefit of their wisdom and experience. They can be especially useful if you are working towards a promotion or need a sounding board in a new job.

A mentor is a more experienced individual willing to share knowledge with someone less experienced in a relationship of mutual trust.

David Clutterbuck

You may already have someone whom you have been using informally as a mentor. This might be an ex-manager, colleague or friend of the family whose advice you have always appreciated.

If you haven't anyone currently, it is worth considering who might be a good sounding board for you in respect of your career. It can be a very informal relationship with the odd coffee here and there; or you can, if they are happy to do so, arrange more regular meetings. However, as the relationship is generally an unpaid one, you will need to be mindful about how much time they may want to commit to mentoring you. If you want a more formal mentoring relationship it's recommended that you discuss expectations right from the outset.

TIP

Some large organisations, such as the civil service for example, may have a formal mentoring scheme in place. You should expect advice, not intervention, from your mentor. Your mentor will not 'fix' things on your behalf.

Tips on working with a mentor
- Find someone you feel you can learn from.
- Agree on what you both want and can give to the relationship.
- Be clear about boundaries – for example their availability, confidentiality, etc.

Many professional associations provide mentoring schemes. For instance MentorSET is a UK-based initiative organised by the Women's Engineering Society and offers a mentoring scheme to help women working in the science, technology, engineering and mathematics industries. Mentoring schemes are often targeted at specific groups of people such as young people, newly qualified professionals in a particular field or certain under-represented groups. Look on the internet for mentoring schemes that may be appropriate for you.

Role models

In Part 2 we looked at the early influence of role models on your personal and career development. Role models can continue to be helpful for you. They may provide inspiration as well as very practical learning. For instance, if you are a female entrepreneur, follow the progress of women in your industry who have set up successful businesses. Read any articles or books they have written. Attend any speaker events where they will be appearing and go and talk to them afterwards. It's always useful to learn from other people who have faced similar challenges to you and emerged on the other side.

Family and friends

Your family and friends will want to help you, but sometimes they are not sure how to. Always share with your loved ones exactly what you are looking for next career-wise. They are the warmest networking contacts you have, but probably the most underused.

I was recently talking to a graduate who wanted to work in the NHS but was finding it difficult to get anywhere. I asked her if she knew of anyone who worked in the NHS. 'Only my sister!' she said as though this didn't count. Following my advice, she asked her sister to put in a word with the HR department and she was offered some work experience which led to her subsequently being chosen for a graduate trainee role in the NHS.

Your loved ones may also be able to help with practical tasks such as checking your CV for errors or choosing an interview outfit. Career transition can be psychologically challenging, so be up-front with them about the emotional support and confidence-building you would find helpful.

If you have a partner, remember that they may be as worried as you about your career situation or indeed have their own career issues they are trying to resolve. The more mutually supportive you can be, the better equipped you will both be to handle any emotional ups and downs that arise.

TIP

Tell your family and friends what you are looking for. Don't assume they know.

Professional career support

You may benefit from working with a career management company to accelerate your career journey by using the additional career services they can provide. These can include career analysis, careers information, job market research services, help devising your self-marketing materials and practical job search support in the implementation of your career plan.

It's especially helpful if you have found it difficult to get high-quality, impartial feedback and advice. Many people also benefit from the regular interaction of working with a coach and the practical and emotional support this provides during a period of transition.

TIP

If you are leaving your company because of redundancy or through a compromise agreement, then ask if they will help pay for career coaching or outplacement support to help you find your next job. There are tax and VAT advantages for you if it is included as part of an exit agreement.

The career coaching industry is unregulated in the UK, so choose a company that adheres to a recognised code of practice for the industry such as the Career Development Institute (CDI). Many companies offer a free initial meeting and this is an excellent opportunity for you to find out more about the company, its staff and its services. Reputable companies will always provide full written information about the services on offer, the resources available and the costs involved. There should never be any secrecy regarding this.

If you are looking for career coaching, check out the Personal Career Management site, www.personalcareermanagement.com, as this will give you a good indication of the kind of services on offer, the standards to expect and likely costs.

Now you've considered who may be able to help you, let's draw up your own contact list.

EXERCISE 43 YOUR CONTACT LIST

1. Write down below a list of people you feel can help you with advice, feedback or potential job contacts. If there are certain individuals you really don't want to approach even if they may have great contacts, perhaps because you have had a difficult relationship in the past, don't bother. However, if you've had a good relationship – what are you waiting for?

2. Highlight those who are most likely to be helpful and arrange to talk to them first.

EXAMPLE

Pete, HR at Pete's company, Dad's company, all the suppliers I worked with, ex-boss, old colleagues at Zenith Enterprises, course tutor, people at church, recruiter who placed me in the job, sister-in-law ...

Greg

Let's now start to implement your career decision! Parts 7 and 8 show you how to market yourself as an ideal candidate for the roles you are interested in and overcome some common career challenges. The final section in Part 9 will bring all of your thoughts and findings together to create a useful career action plan and career insights guide that will keep you focused on your career goals and help you track progress.

PART 7

The art of self-promotion

The job market is always highly competitive. You have to be able to convince an employer that you are a great candidate for the job if you are to get the opportunities you want and deserve. This section provides practical advice on how to maximise the effectiveness of your self-marketing and make yourself easy to hire.

In this section we will:

■ understand what employers want

■ decode job adverts

■ discuss CVs, applications and social media

■ explore the workings of recruitment agencies and headhunters

■ consider other job search strategies

■ identify key interview techniques

■ consider self-employment

■ learn about other specific career challenges.

20 MAKING YOUR-SELF EASY TO HIRE

Whatever your career aspirations, you have to be able to talk positively about yourself to others if you want to be hired for the roles you are interested in.

This is trickier than it looks. From childhood we are brought up to believe that anything that borders on self-promotion is 'big-headed' and risks commiting a social faux pas. Within organisations we are encouraged to talk about the 'we' of the team rather than 'I', so that we downplay our individual contribution and elevate the team ethos. No wonder many people feel uncomfortable when it comes to 'selling themselves' to potential employers – they're not used to it.

However, in the job market you are going to be faced with complete strangers asking you detailed and intrusive questions about all aspects of your professional capabilities and personality. You have such a short window of time to impress people, a quick glance at your CV, an hour-long interview and the recruiters are already making judgements rightly or wrongly about your suitability depending on what you say and how you say it.

This is why it's so important that you understand how to present yourself positively as a candidate, both on paper and in person. This doesn't mean pretending to be someone you are not. It's more about presenting the very best version of yourself with all the relevant information the recruiter needs to make an informed decision.

This section is going to show you how to do this to increase your chances of being shortlisted and offered the job you want.

What does the employer want?

Regardless of the role and organisation, there are some common features about what employers regard as an ideal employee. Let's look at their wish list.

Are you realistic about the job?

A surprisingly large number of candidates apply for jobs without understanding what the job actually entails. Carefully read the job adverts and job descriptions and do your research so you have a down-to-earth view of what is involved. Any differences in your expectations and the employers will severely reduce your chances of being selected.

Do you genuinely want the job?

Candidates who appear genuinely interested in the job are more attractive because they are more likely to be highly motivated and to stay. If you seem ambivalent or laid back about whether you get the job or not, then the recruiter is likely to suspect, probably quite rightly, that you will leave as soon as you get a better job offer. Don't play it cool – play it keen!

Are you a high-performer?

Employers want staff who are self-motivated and energetic and who will get things done to a high standard. They want to hear about your successes, where you have used your skills and initiative to meet demanding goals without getting distracted, bogged down or discouraged. If you've been successful in the past then they will see this as a good prediction for how you will perform in their own company.

Will you add value?

It's expensive to recruit and employ staff. Employers want to know that it is going to be worth it. Candidates who show that they have made a positive contribution to their organisation will be easier to hire because they are seen as more of an asset than a cost. They will be interested to hear of any examples where you have helped make improvements whether it is business efficiencies, enhancing quality standards, building new commercial relationships or generating new ideas.

Are you reliable and resilient?

Employers want trustworthy, dependable staff who are able to cope under pressure, whether they are dealing with a demanding workload, a difficult workplace relationship or an unforeseen problem situation. They want someone who is calm, resilient and a safe pair of hands and they will use the interview situation and occasionally some pre-interview tests to check how you perform under pressure.

Are you a good representative for the company?

Employers invest a lot of time and energy in building a positive reputation and the last thing they want is for that to be deliberately or inadvertently sabotaged by a rogue employee. They want to feel that they can trust you to be professional, behave appropriately and that your approach is in line with the impression the company is trying to convey to the wider world.

Will you get on with people?

Whether it is working collaboratively within a team, dealing with customers or others, your ability to work well with others is going to be important. So be very careful about sharing any negative information about employers or individuals you have worked with as the recruiter may wonder what the other side of the story is and whether in fact it was you that was the problem.

Will you be flexible?

Employers like candidates who are collaborative rather than territorial. They also want staff who can adjust to the constantly changing demands of the organisation rather than being rigid. If you can show that you have a growth mindset, able to deal positively with challenges and tackle things that are difficult, then they are more likely to see you as someone who can grow with the organisation's needs.

Are you going to fit in?

If you are applying to a particular organisation then you have to research the company culture so you can anticipate the in-house style. The manager will also be assessing whether they feel they could work well with you. However, if you can reassure the employer that you can do the job and in addition meet all of the criteria for an ideal employee, then you are more likely to be seen as someone who will fit in.

The ideal employee

Can do the job	Business savvy
Realistic about the job	Uses initiative/innovator
Genuinely wants the job	Ambassador for the company
Motivated	Team player
Resilient	Quality conscious
Reliable	Customer focused
Realistic	Up to date
Trustworthy	Will fit in
Results focused	Interpersonal skills
Action-orientated	Professional

21 APPLYING FOR ADVERTISED ROLES

Great – you have seen a job that you want to apply for and you are keen to get your application in as soon as possible. However, before you quickly upload your CV and press the button, there are a number of things you can do to increase the chances of being on that shortlist pile.

- Use a highlighter pen to mark the candidate requirements outlined in the job advert, job description and person specification form. This includes *all* of the key selection criteria – both essential and desirable as you need to address all of these in your application.
- Look at the company's website to get a feel for the culture of the organisation and how they talk about themselves. Are they fast-paced, ethical, customer-focused, looking for rapid growth or keen to promote their reputation as a safe pair of hands?
- Check out their competitors to see how they contrast and compare.
- Research company news, PR releases, Facebook and LinkedIn company pages to find out what is preoccupying the organisation at the moment, any plans, threats, concerns, expansions, etc.
- Talk to people you know who work for this organisation or in this area for inside information that might be of help.

You can then use this information to tailor your CV and applications by:

- showing them right at the start of your application that you have what they want, for example specific expertise or sector background. Downplay other areas of your career experience that may seem a distraction to them.
- finding parallels between your organisation and theirs especially if you are looking to change sector, for example 'Used to working in a similarly target-driven environment'.

> Your applications should focus on the things that are of most importance to the employer rather than simply being a record of all the things you have ever done. For instance if they want someone with specific IT skills, then talk about all the experience you have of this right at the start of your CV and at interview, even if you've done less of this more recently.
>
> **Jane Garrard, career coach**

- being the person they want. If they want someone who is used to delivering a high quality service, or is creative or a great communicator then give them some examples to prove that you are that person.
- tailoring your language. Reflect back some of the exact words they use in the job details. For example they may use words such as 'customer delight' or 'design thinking' and if you can sprinkle these into your application, showing that you understand what they mean and have direct experience of working in this way, then this will reinforce your suitability. Be careful about using jargon or in-house terms that they may not be familiar with.

As an example let's look at two job adverts for a Financial Controller taken from the https://jobs.telegraph.co.uk and www.gaapweb.com job boards. They have both outlined very similar tasks and responsibilities such as management accounts, budgeting and forecasting. However there are a number of clues in the advert that indicate important differences in the kind of candidate they want.

Role 1

Financial Controller – £35–£45k dependent on experience

This role provides a direct opportunity to shape business strategy, as well as challenge the commercial teams. The company is a well-established and respected manufacturing business providing solutions for a multitude of prominent brands with plans to grow their impressive span of product ranges over the coming years.

Our company culture is friendly, inclusive and allows employees to have a hands-on role in the running of the business. As such, this role will suit a personable individual who is excellent at building relationships. They must have a friendly yet hard-working attitude, be diligent, reliable, and a real team player who wants to grow with the business. This will suit either a formally qualified accountant or one with a wealth of industry experience but no official qualification, ideally with a manufacturing background.

Role 2

Financial Controller – £36k–£45k + benefits

A newly created opportunity for a Financial Controller working for a growing SME business looking after a team of three across financial and management accounts, process improvement and systems. We are seeking an experienced accountant who can bring their own ideas to the table of how to improve and develop staff and systems within the organisation and who can be a leader of change within the role.

You will be working with both finance and non-finance stakeholders so will need to be an articulate communicator and strong influencer across the wider business and able to deal with change at a swift pace. The business is an owner-managed SME which is looking to expand in the next couple of years with potential businesses lined up for potential acquisitions. You will have strong management reporting experience and be a qualified accountant (ACA/ACCA/CIMA). Ideally you will also have worked closely with owner/managers in an SME previously.

Now let's compare the two in more detail to gauge who their ideal candidate may be. This process will show you the level of thought needed when interpreting adverts.

Role 1

Financial Controller – £35–£45k dependent on experience

This role provides an opportunity to shape business strategy, as well as challenge the commercial teams. The company is a well-established and respected manufacturing businesses providing solutions for a multitude of prominent brands with plans to grow their impressive span of product ranges over the coming years.

Our company culture is friendly, inclusive and allows employees to have a hands-on role in the running of the business. As such, this role will suit a personable individual who is excellent at building relationships. They must have a friendly yet hard-working attitude, be diligent, reliable, and a real team player who wants to grow with the business. This will suit either a formally qualified accountant or one with a wealth of industry experience but no official qualification, ideally with a manufacturing background.

I've highlighted some of the keywords in this advert which gives hints as to what they are looking for. There are some keywords that stand out: 'friendly, inclusive, personable, building relationships'. Clearly the company culture here is one very much of team work with employees treated as important contributors to the business rather than just a labour cost. They are looking for someone with the interpersonal skills to work in this more democratically inclusive environment so it certainly wouldn't suit anyone who is more status conscious or prefers to work in a more rigid hierarchy. It does talk about the candidate having the ability to challenge the commercial teams, but everything in this advert suggests that they want someone who can do this in a way that is respectful and who has a very strong team player orientation.

This means that when applying for the role it would be a good idea to emphasise your team working, various collaborations and constructive working relationships, and how you have contributed to business goals by using influencing skills rather than confrontation.

They are open to someone without formal accountancy qualifications but clearly this needs to be offset by lots of appropriate financial experience within the manufacturing sector. It's obvious that they want someone with a manufacturing background so you need to emphasise any experience at all you have in that area, even if it was a very long time ago in a quite different role. They want to know you understand some of the culture of working in this sector, like perhaps lean or agile working, the focus on productivity and cost control, quality standards, logistics, health and safety, team working as well as an understanding of future trends such as technological change and how this might affect manufacturing businesses for the future.

Role 2

Financial Controller – £36k to £45k + benefits

An opportunity for a Financial Controller working for a growing SME business looking after a team of three across financial and management accounts, process improvement and systems. We are seeking an experienced accountant who can bring their own ideas to the table of how to improve and develop staff and systems within the organisation and who can be a leader of change within the role.

You will be working with both finance and non-finance stakeholders so will need to be an articulate communicator and strong influencer across the wider business and able to deal with change at a swift pace. The business is an owner-managed SME which is looking to expand in the next couple of years with potential businesses lined up for potential acquisitions. You will have strong management reporting experience and be a qualified accountant (ACA/ACCA/CIMA). Ideally you will also have worked closely with owner/managers in an SME previously.

This second role is for an experienced accountant with formal qualifications. It focuses on managing a finance team so they will want to know more about your staff management capabilities and experience, but what also comes through loud and clear in this advert is that they want the candidate to be a change agent – and to be able to do this at a 'swift pace'. It's important to them that you can identify ideas for improving systems and processes – business efficiencies, cost reductions, etc, and get these up and running quickly. In addition, the owner is looking to make acquisitions so any previous experience of this would be an advantage and therefore should be mentioned in full in your application especially if you have been involved in identifying and evaluating business opportunities, valuations, financing arrangements, due diligence and negotiations, etc.

The company is an SME owner-managed business which brings to your attention that the boss is likely to be much more heavily invested both financially and emotionally with the business than a CEO who is a hired hand. This means that it will be even more important that the owner feels they can trust you and that your approach is compatible with theirs. It would definitely be a good idea to do some digging around to see what you can find out about the owner so you can anticipate their style.

Your application for this role needs to focus on team management, business improvement, acquisitions experience and a style likely to appeal to the CEO, in addition to outlining your technical qualifications and expertise.

Once you have gleaned all the information you can from the advert, it's time to look closely at the job description and person specification which will tell you the selection criteria the employers will use to assess your application. Let's choose a different job to examine this.

Example of a person specification for an administrator

Selection criteria	Essential	Desirable	Means of assessment
Education and qualifications	Educated to GCSE level standard or equivalent with strong proficiency in English and Maths		CV
Skills and experience	Strong skills in Microsoft Office (Word, Excel, PowerPoint, Outlook) Previous experience of working as an administrator	Experience of working with Salesforce database	CV/interview

	Excellent written and verbal communication skills		
Personal qualities	Ability to work under pressure Good team player Problem-solver		CV/interview

In your application you will need to prove your capabilities for every single criteria, both the *desirable* and the *essential* items. In the above example this means that in your application you also need to include any experience you have with Salesforce.

If you don't have everything they are looking for then there is no point just ignoring it and hoping they won't notice – because they will. For instance for the job above, they would ideally like to appoint a candidate with some experience of using a Salesforce CRM database. If you don't have that experience then you must show why this wouldn't be a problem. Perhaps you have worked with other types of databases and used these in the past to input data and run reports in a similar way to Salesforce. In addition, check out this database system on line or talk to somebody who uses it who can talk you through it. Mention all of these mitigating factors in your application.

Proving yourself in your applications

- Address *all* the selection criteria in the person specification form and advert.
- Provide specific examples where you have used the skills and experience directly related to this line of work and they have added value to the organization.
- List relevant qualifications or training that indicate you have the technical skills and knowledge needed and you are up to date.
- Detail previous experience working in a similar type of organisation or sector even if it was a while ago.
- Give examples of experience working with similar internal/external customers or clients.
- Illustrate that you have the personal qualities of a highly professional, model employee.

22 HOW TO GET YOUR CV ON THE SHORT-LIST PILE

Most recruiters will spend an average of about 10 seconds reading your CV before deciding whether it will be rejected or moved to the shortlist pile. You've got even less time with the digital recruitment software used by many large employers and recruitment agencies to filter applications. This software literally takes nanoseconds to analyse the text in your CV and then produce a prioritised list of candidates for the recruiter. This chapter will show you how to ensure your CV works well for both human and digital filtering processes.

So what should I put in my CV?

A CV should normally be two pages in length. This should give you enough space to include lots of good relevant content while forcing you to keep it succinct and focused. On occasions you may need to go onto three pages, especially if your career has been project-based, or you want to list things you have written or produced. Let's look at how you can use that space to good effect.

Personal information

Write your name and contact details at the top of your CV to make it easy for the recruiter to contact you. You don't need to write your full address but you should include the area you live in or postcode and any other specific areas where you could work (e.g. Leeds and London) so that recruiters can see which work locations are realistic for you. If you leave your location blank then you may be ignored by recruiters searching the database for candidates located in a particular area.

You should also state your legal rights to work in the UK if you think that a recruiter could have any query about your eligibility.

Write a personal profile

This is a great way to show very early on why you are such a great candidate. It consists of about four to five sentences placed directly under your contact details. Describe yourself in similar terms to those the recruiter uses in their job details. For instance if the advert says they are looking for a 'Team leader' then call yourself this in your CV profile even if your actual job title is 'Team Supervisor'. Job titles vary so much between organisations that it is acceptable to label yourself slightly differently in your profile as long as you can justify the content of the jobs are similar. The advantage in doing this is that it positions you, right from the start, as someone who seems a good fit.

State how many years' experience you have in a relevant role, profession or sector to emphasise your credibility. If you are relatively new to the world of work then it's fine to describe yourself instead as 'Recent graduate' or 'Apprentice' so they understand why your CV features less experience.

Employers want to understand the seniority and level of responsibility at which you have been operating so they need information on the scale and complexity of the work you have been involved in. Share data which you think can help impress the recruiter such as the total value of the accounts you are responsible for, the number of projects or product lines you work on or the amount of queries or customers you deal with in a week. Choose examples which demonstrate that you have sizeable responsibility without of course sharing confidential business information.

Professional or educational qualifications should always be mentioned in the career profile if they are directly relevant to the job you are applying for, for example a Computer Science degree, BTech in Design or certificate in HR management. These clearly show your credentials to do the job.

Refer briefly to an achievement or other positive contribution, which you can expand on later in your CV. Maybe you won an award for employee of the month, exceeded your annual sales targets, built new partnerships, turned around an underperforming team or brought order to what was previously a chaotic system.

If you have worked on any prestigious projects, with high profile brands, world-class organisations or VIPs then name-drop these into your profile as you gain kudos by association.

Candidates often use the profile to describe the kind of person they are but this will sound like a cliché unless it is directly relevant to the role you are applying for **and** you back it up with evidence. For instance, if you are

Graduate with limited work experience

Elliot Mills
Address: 3, The Chalfonts, SL9 089
Email: elliot@googlemail.com
Mobile: 0775 557 555

State that you are looking for a career in marketing if applying for a marketing job

Recent graduate in Cultural Studies seeking to develop a career in marketing to help brands and organisations attract new customers and build customer loyalty. Experience includes working with marketing agencies to help with research and customer insights. Strong visual creativity, includings producing my own artwork. Excellent interpersonal skills as shown by my work at exhibitions where I have to quickly build rapport with visitors to encourage them to visit the company's stand. Excellent knowledge of social media marketing platforms and advanced IT skills including Microsoft Office and Adobe Suite. Proficient on both Windows and Mac.

Clear that you are a recent graduate so they know your work experience will be limited

Using profile to show that you have the skills and personality traits that are very relevant for marketing

Relevant skills and experience:

- Marketing Intern with the branding agency 'ABC' where I shadowed the Creative Director and assisted with brand research, photo-shoots and competitor surveys. My report on competitors was used as the basis for a presentation by the Creative Director
- Marketing work placement for XYZ, a creative marketing agency where I assisted on the research for the planning discussions for a new government health promotion campaign
- Promotions experience including working on exhibition stands at Olympia where I was tasked with enticing people to the stand, promoting the products and filtering the warm leads to the senior sales person. They were so pleased with my work that they asked me to come back for three subsequent exhibitions
- Marketing the university hockey club at freshers week, where I designed original artwork for the stall's banners and leaflets and created a 'bully-off' competition, which was great fun and drew people to the stall. We posted people's scores on social media to keep people engaged and track interest so that we could follow this up later
- Working in hospitality where I multi-tasked between acting as the barman, waiter and porter in a small but very busy hotel, ensuring that guests felt a five-star welcome at all times
- Strong artistic abilities including graphic design, photography and fine art. I have produced and sold my own digital and watercolour artworks including commissions and my work has been displayed at art festivals

IT skills important for this role

Evidence that you did a good job and they were pleased you're your work

Positive words used throughout e.g. five-star, strong

Career history:

Intern Marketing Assistant   ABC Agency   February 2017

- Researching competitors for a sales pitch to a client. This involved in-depth internet research using many different sources and contacting the competitors directly for information. The Creative Director incorporated this information into their sales pitch presentation
- Organising props and liaising with the model agency for the photoshoot
- Attending ideas generation meetings for an upcoming client presentation
- Taking notes of meetings and circulating these as minutes
- Ad hoc tasks such as welcoming visitors, running errands, etc

Even though this was very limited experience talked positively about it and made the most of it

Marketing Assistant   XYZ Agency   November 2016

Showing an
understanding
of analytic
processes in
marketing

- Researched statistics on accidents where mobile phone use was attributed as contributing cause. This involved using many different sources including the health and safety executive, police reports and accident and emergency reports
- Gathered together five tragic news stories that illustrated the mobile phone problem
- Interviewed members of the general public on their perception of the dangers of mobile phone use, highlighting key quotes that I felt would be of interest and codifying my answers for the subsequent data analysis

Marketing Promotions   Exhibitions Olympia   August–Oct 2015

- Brand ambassador for diverse companies including Spark Health Foods, Altipro software and Demagne Hotel
- Handing out promotional material, encouraging visitors to come to the stand, providing information about the products, capturing their contact information and filtering warm leads to the sales team

Drawing out
the relevance
of this
experience to
marketing

General Assistant The Hotel   2016 to date

- Front of house staff at a hotel where I worked weekends and helped out with anything that was necessary, from working in the bar, to being the porter and helping in emergencies such as arranging for medical help when a guest fell ill and rescuing a guest's belongings when a bathroom overflowed
- Always ensuring that guests were received courteously and served efficiently so that their stay was an enjoyable one

Showing model
employee:
willing,
customer-
focused, calm
under pressure

Custom artworks business   2014 to date

- I enjoy creating digital graphic art and photography. This is mainly as a hobby however I have been commissioned to produce digital art pieces by family, friends and two local businesses. I created all the marketing materials for the hockey stall at freshers week and my photography and other work have also appeared in local arts festivals

Showing
relevance of
your hobby
to marketing
career

Education:
The University (2014–2017)   BA in Cultural Studies (2.i)

Dissertation (Research Project) Title: The Role of Art in Times of Societal Conflict.

The High School, Everytowns (2008–2014)

A levels: Fine Art (A), Photography (B), English (C)
GCSEs: 9 grades A-C

Graduates
employers are
interested in
your hobbies
so give them a
flavour of what
you enjoy

Interests:
Art, photography, hockey, travelling (4-month trip to South Asia in 2016)

Functional CV (A career changer. A teacher who wants to move into a museum education role)

Molly Malone
1 The Garden, LE32 4JY
07777 555
mm@gmail.com

Highly creative, PGCE-qualified History Education Professional with substantial expertise in providing fun, engaging, inclusive and informative learning experiences motivated by my deep passion for bringing history to life. My active learning approach includes using artwork and digital interactivity to help students understand key themes, dramatic role play and story-telling to provoke discussion about historical figures and their motivations, and gamification by developing fun quizzes, activity trails and history bingo. As a teaching professional I bring an in-depth understanding of the needs of different learners, up-to-date knowledge of the school curriculum and a strong insight into how museums can best support and encourage student curiosity and learning objectives.

Relevant skills and experience:

- Praised in the last school OFSTED report for the creativity of our history teaching and its flexibility in working with students with SEN needs
- Developed a highly successful and innovative inter-generational, local history project where the pupils interviewed members of the local community and developed materials for an exhibition about WW2 including video footage, posters and original artefacts. This was so well received that the exhibition was mounted in the local council offices and at the local village fair
- Built very strong links with the British Museum and the Imperial War Museum, as well as local historical sites like the Chiltern Open Air Museum to create bespoke learning itineraries for our curriculum learning objectives.
- Created an X Factor competition of historical characters where students dressed in costume to compete for the title of most influential British figure in history
- Developed and curated a range of different learning materials such as fun quizzes, memory joggers and history mind maps to reinforce learning
- Created a 'Who do you think you are' project where students researched their own family history and this became part of a digital social history archive for the local community. Enlisted the help of parents, libraries, local History Association and national archives all working in collaboration. The contributions were fantastic
- Developed weekly 'show and tell' where pupils asked to bring in a historical artefact which they have researched and give a presentation about its history
- Used art and music of the period, costumes and imitation artefacts to set the scene for lessons. E.g. Tudor period, English Civil War and WW1
- Committee member for local Chalfont History Society where I have actively been involved in uncovering records, assigning information plaques around the village and creating with local families an aural record of reminiscences and personal histories
- Created a daily 'On this Day in History' where we look at what happened today. The kids always remember what happened on their birthday

Margin notes:

Rather than using the title 'teacher', uses 'Education Professional' as more aligned with job applied for; avoids being labelled as teacher right from the start

Keying in to what they want museum educator to do and providing details of approach and experience

Knowledge of learning curriculum and teachers' needs very important for this role

Evidence of external endorsement

Great examples of creating history learning projects which are very appropriate for museum educator

Positive words, e.g. fun, well-received, fantastic

Example of original social history research

- Created a historical walking tour of the village, with students taking photos of locations, writing the information for visitors, creating an interactive map. Developed this as a website page where people could add their additional information as a collaborative village effort

History Teacher:

Brook School   2013 – present

Detailing career history on the second page which is as a teacher rather than as a museum educator

Detailing the approach which is very relevant for museum education roles

- Planning and teaching the history curriculum for KS3 and KS4. This involved setting clear objectives, detailed lesson planning, devising materials, close co-ordination with my colleagues and the school timetable as well as student marketing, assessments and progress reviews with students and parents
- Developing multi-disciplinary, active learning approaches with students leading presentations, small group problem-solving, using IT, games, drama and experiential learning strategies
- Working closely with specialists in gender and diversity, educational psychologists, school counsellors and SENCO to enhance accessibility and support for a very wide range of learners with different needs
- Leading contributor to the continuing professional development of the history team, sharing knowledge on subject expertise, best practice in teaching, co-coaching and mentoring two newly qualified members of staff

Need for museum educator to know about inclusive learning for different audiences

Meadow School   2008–2013

- Teaching history at KS3
- Built constructive relationships with students with social and behavioural challenges who found the classroom environment difficult but who went on to make good academic progress in history
- Increased the take-up of GCSE history by students choosing their subjects in Year 9

Showing that you have enthused people about history which is key feature of museum educator role

Education and qualifications:

- Post-Graduate Certificate in Education – Challoners College, 2007
- BA – History – York 2006
- A Levels in History (A), English (A) and RE (B)
- 7 subjects at O Level including Maths and English

Additional Training:

Outstanding Teaching in History, Engaging the Disengaged, The Inclusive Classroom, Accelerated Learning, Embedding Outstanding Teaching, Diversity Awareness, Child Protection Awareness training

Ongoing professional development shows credibility and commitment to own learning, and many of the courses are very relevant for an education professional

TIP

Find lots more information and templates in my book *You're Hired! How to write a brilliant CV.*

23 HOW TO USE SOCIAL MEDIA FOR YOUR CAREER

Social media is a fantastic vehicle for sharing information online, finding out about others and interacting with them. No wonder recruiters increasingly use it. They still advertise roles to attract candidates but they also use professionally focused social media sites such as LinkedIn to directly approach candidates whose online profiles are of interest to them. They will also Google you before interview to see if there is any online information, usually from the social media sites, that might reinforce or perhaps even invalidate your attractiveness as a candidate. Social media is an important opportunity for you to create a professional profile that will positively influence hiring decision-makers so let's look at how you can best use it to your advantage.

LinkedIn

Regarding your career, the most important site for you to use currently is LinkedIn which has over 467 million members. This is used by professionals from all occupations and sectors to let the world know about their capabilities and background. It provides opportunities for you to build connections with others with shared interests. In the digital age, where the first contact you may have with someone is online rather than in person, it becomes especially important to manage your online reputation so that it conveys the messages you want to communicate.

Here are tips to help make the most of this resource.

Positive advertisement. Your LinkedIn profile should be built on the same principles as your CV. It needs to be a very positive advertisement for you and very relevant to the audience you are trying to impress. Make it achievement focused rather than just a list of your duties and responsibilities. Include details of awards you have won, targets exceeded, significant contributions you have made. If your CV works well for you then you can just cut and paste a shorter version of it into your LinkedIn profile.

Keywords. Look at the selection criteria for the type of job or project you might be interested in next and tick these as your key skills when you complete your profile. Then use these same keywords sprinkled within your profile and employment history so that recruiters using these search terms can easily find you, for instance labelling yourself as 'Marketing Manager with FMCG background'. LinkedIn will also notify you of jobs that it thinks you will be interested in depending on the job titles and keywords you use within your profile.

Be truthful. Remember that your LinkedIn profile is in the public domain so all information shared must be accurate otherwise you might be challenged by someone who knows otherwise. Prospective employers will also check for discrepancies between your CV and LinkedIn profile.

No holiday snaps. Include a photo but make sure that it is business appropriate rather than a holiday snap.

Testimonials. Rather like Amazon reviews, there is the facility to add personal recommendations from people who have worked with you. These testimonials help build your credibility – as it is evidence that people who have worked with you think that you were excellent. Ask people you know who will be happy to write good things about you, for example your manager, colleagues, customers, etc.

Multimedia. Unlike a conventional CV you can also add to your LinkedIn profile links to any other multimedia materials that you have produced that you feel illustrate your skills and achievements, such as published articles, videos, PowerPoint presentations, creative portfolios, or your website or blog.

Build connections. The wider your network the more likely you are to hear about opportunities. LinkedIn will generate suggestions of people you may want to connect with, either because you both worked in the same place at the same time, went to the same school or you are both members of a shared group. You don't have to join every group, or invite everyone you know, nor are you under any obligation to accept anyone else's invitation. It's fine to be selective but do actively build your network beyond your immediate circle.

Research. If you are interested in a particular company, then you can follow their LinkedIn organisation page for updates and also search through LinkedIn to see if you know anyone working there who can make an introduction for you or talk to you about the company. You can also find out more about the career backgrounds of your interview panel before you meet them.

Activity updates. Use these as part of your own personal PR campaign to remind people about you and what you can offer. For instance share news about any business successes, events or feedback from a happy customer. You can also send out comments or questions on current topics to encourage a dialogue with people in your network. These act as a gentle nudge to remind people of who you are and what you do.

Join LinkedIn groups. There are thousands of different groups on the site. Recruiters, employers and managers will also be members of this group and will be visiting these groups if they are looking for new staff.

Twitter

Twitter is a much more informal platform than LinkedIn and as it can be used for both personal and professional reasons, it's especially important that you are careful not to blur boundaries. You don't necessarily want your social banter or political rants being read by a prospective employer. Either be very careful what you post or create a couple of different twitter accounts with only the professional one being identifiably you in the bio.

Twitter profile. Create a professional-looking Twitter profile explaining who you are and what you do. You'll need to be succinct as you only have 160 characters to describe yourself.

Activity updates. As with your LinkedIn activity updates, you can use Twitter as part of a personal PR campaign to remind people of your expertise, share successes or interesting articles.

Be a follower. You can 'follow' individuals, companies and recruitment agencies to keep up to date with their latest news and vacancies. When you follow someone they will look at your profile so it's a good way to get their attention.

Messaging. Send individuals and companies you are interested in working or collaborating with a message of appreciation or constructive comment about some shared topic. It can be the start of building a relationship and will position you well if you subsequently apply for a job with them.

Job listings. You can search for jobs on Twitter. When you add a hashtag symbol '#' directly in front of a word, a link is created and if you type this into the Twitter search bar you can find the tweets containing this keyword. This is very useful when you want to search for jobs, for example #ITjobs or #marketingjob. Play around with the search terms you use to see what gives you the best results, for example '#job #HR #London'.

Beware your digital footprint

Employers will often Google you and look at your social media profiles even if they have asked you to apply for a vacancy via CV or online application. They want to verify that the information you have submitted is correct and consistent and see if they can discover anything else about you that could influence their hiring decision. It's important that you know what they are seeing. Are you easy to find and, if so, is the information that surfaces about you likely to reassure an employer or could it put them off? If there is anything online that could put you in a negative light then delete it.

Informality. It's a very relaxed, supposedly more spontaneous form of communication and people will abbreviate or miss out words to fit their message into the 140 characters. However, be careful about your spelling and the way in which you express yourself because an employer who sees your public tweets will be judging whether they think this is compatible with the public image they, as a company, are trying to present.

Facebook

This is still primarily a site for social reasons. However, there are some ways in which it can be helpful for your career too.

Use your social network. Family and friends are a very under-utilised resource when it comes to tapping into advice and information. They generally want to be helpful so sharing your career with them in person and via your Facebook account encourages a conversation where they can offer insights and perhaps links to people they know who work in the area you are interested in.

Company pages. These pages tend to be great interactive information resources featuring news, features and often someone who will answer your online questions.

Clear boundaries. it is best to keep your Facebook account private and open only to friends and family. If you open it up to colleagues and professional acquaintances, do you really want them to be able to read your Facebook comments or those of your extended network? Be careful about boundaries.

Other social media sites

There are many other social media sites that can be helpful for your career such as Google+, niche forums such as the Guardian Teachers Network or Stack Overflow for software programmers. These sites are evolving all the time. However similar principles apply: create a public profile that presents you positively for the roles you are interested in, be careful about sharing anything contentious that is under your own name and use it to connect with others.

Maintenance

It can be time-consuming to regularly update all your social media profiles with your activity. Applications such as tweetdeck or hootsuite enable you to more easily manage all your social media applications from one place.

Social media checklist

- Make it a positive advert for you.
- Use relevant keywords to increase your visibility.
- Be truthful – it's public.
- Connect with others.
- Use it to research and find other people who might be useful.
- Keep your profile active by sharing activity updates, comments, etc.
- Keep personal and professional comments separate.

24 HANDLING RECRUITMENT AGENCIES AND HEADHUNTERS

What's the difference between a recruitment agency and a headhunting outfit or what is sometimes called an executive search firm? Some firms seem to use this term interchangeably but the main difference is primarily in how each firm sources their candidates and how they get paid.

Recruitment agencies tend to use adverts and their own CV databases to find candidates they think the employer will be interested in. They are often in competition with other agencies, which is why you often see the same job advertised by different consultancies. Only the agency that supplies the successful candidate will get paid by the employer which is why they work quickly to get good candidates to the employer as soon as possible.

Headhunters or executive search firms are usually the only firm engaged by the employer and they are paid to proactively find individuals who fit the employers' brief regardless of whether the individual is actively looking for a job or not. Headhunters tend to be used for more senior or niche/harder to fill roles and they usually get paid for different stages of the recruitment process, for example initial research, shortlisting, interviews, selection testing and appointment.

If you are looking for your next job then you should make sure that you are visible to agencies and headhunters by uploading your CV or completing the online application form for the websites and agencies who operate in your field, for instance www.totallylegal.com for legal jobs.

Also ring up their offices and ask for a meeting. Some recruiters are more diligent in meeting with their candidates than others but they are more likely to arrange this if you present yourself as a highly employable candidate who they think they can easily place or you match a particular role they are working towards fulfilling at the moment. Don't be offended if they don't want to meet or they don't return your calls. They work to such high pressure sales targets that they may not have time to meet you unless they want to talk to you about a specific opportunity.

Recruitment agencies

Manage your expectations. Their customer is the employer not you. So if you expect them to spend time promoting you, coaching you, looking after you, or even protecting your best interests when it's contrary to their own, then unfortunately you are likely to be disappointed.

Be an easy sell. You are more likely to be a preferred candidate for them if you are clear and realistic about what you want next, have created a good CV and seem interview ready. If you are looking for a career change, then you will have to convince them why you are better than more obvious candidates before they will consider putting you forward. The agency is being judged by the employer on the appropriateness of the candidates they supply so they tend to play it safe.

Respond quickly. The agency may be competing to get their candidates considered ahead of those of a rival agency and too slow a response to an agency's telephone call or email may mean you have already lost the opportunity.

> Candidates assume sometimes that if you send a CV to a recruiter or headhunter that they will find you a job. But that's not their business model. You're a route to their revenue but their paying client is the employer not you and this is where their attention will be focused. So don't take it personally if they say you are not right for them or don't return your call.
>
> **Jo Thurman, *career coach***

Recruiter databases. When uploading your CV or online application to an agency's database ensure that it includes lots of appropriate keywords relevant to the job and sector. These keywords will be used by the recruiter to select candidates with the right expertise from the database.

Go for roles that you want. While the recruitment agent may be very persuasive, do not be pressured into considering a role that you know you don't want. It is a waste of time for everyone concerned if you are put forward for a role that you are unlikely to accept.

Job briefing. The agency may initially be reluctant to give you job details as they don't want you to contact the company without them involved as this could cut them out of their commission. However, before you go for the interview, ask the recruiter for all the information they can share including job details, salary range, company culture, etc, as you will need these details to prepare.

Salary requirements. You can discuss this in advance with your agency and they will have some good advice on market rates. They are usually happy to liaise with the company to try and raise the salary if they can because they are often paid a percentage of the potential annual salary.

Dealing with headhunters

Headhunters are notoriously elusive, often preferring to find you rather than you come to them. However, there are some practical things you can do to increase your chances of getting headhunted and, once through the door, make the right impression.

Digital presence. You must have a strong online presence and join social networking sites such as LinkedIn to promote your business profile, as these are regularly trawled by headhunters looking to source good candidates.

Expert status. Position yourself as an industry/sector expert by writing articles, sitting on professional committees, becoming involved in your professional institute, speaking at conferences and applying for awards so that you build up a reputation wider than just your organization.

Network extensively. In their research headhunters ask people for recommendations of suitable candidates so the more people who know you and what you are good at, the more likely it is that your name will surface.

Name-drop. Ask around your network for the name of headhunters they have worked with either as a candidate or employer and ask if you can use their name to facilitate an introduction with them.

Take a long-term view. It may be several months, even sometimes years, before they approach you with a suitable job, but when they do, you want to make sure that you hear about it. Keep in touch with them via LinkedIn so they hear regular updates about your career progress.

Always take the call. Always be willing to listen whether you are considering a career move or not. If it is not right for you at that time you may be able to refer on someone within your network for whom it would be ideal.

Know what you want. It's important that you are clear with them on what you consider to be a good career move – they won't want to waste their or the employer's time if you don't think the opportunity is right for you.

Don't spill the secrets. While an informal chat over coffee may seem very relaxing, always remember that they are being paid by the employer to check you out and they've a duty to share anything that might be material. Don't say anything that you wouldn't say at an interview with the employer – keep it positive.

Target the relevant person in the headhunting practice. If you are approaching a large headhunter's firm, then there will usually be a person specialising in your area and you should approach them directly rather than sending a general letter or email. Their details are usually on their website or you can just ring up and ask.

Be interview-ready. When you meet with the headhunter be well prepared, smartly presented and confident. They want to put forward candidates who can do the job but who also can perform well at interview.

Never lie or exaggerate. Headhunters are paid to check you out with previous employers, including talking to colleagues to find out about your reputation, your reason for leaving, etc. They will do extensive checks sometimes before they even meet with you and they are often better than the employer at sniffing out any inconsistencies in your stories.

Beware the fakes

Despite very clear guidelines from the REC (Recruitment and Employment Confederation) there are some unscrupulous practices in the job market. This includes advertising fake jobs to attract new CVs so that an agency can extend its candidate database. If an agency knows that you are actively job-seeking they can also note your employer as a potential sales prospect once you have left.

The signs of a fake job are usually that it seems to be too good to be true. It is likely to be paid above normal market rates, can be based from anywhere and the selection criteria seems to be so loose that it could fit candidates from a very wide range of backgrounds. The moment you ring up to enquire about it or upload your CV you are told that the post has been filled, although you will often see the same advert resurface at a later date. This is a classic fake job.

Equally, as a candidate you should never have to part with any money to a recruitment agency. It is unlawful for anyone to charge you a fee or a commission to get you a job. The only exception is in the entertainment and modelling sector where this might be part of a management fee.

25 SPECULATIVE APPROACHES AND THE UNADVERTISED JOB MARKET

Responding to adverts is not the only way to find your next role. An estimated 60 to 70% of jobs are recruited via other means including candidates being personally recommended to the company, hearing about opportunities through networking and individuals proactively contacting companies and managers to offer their services. I've worked with many individuals from CEOs to personal assistants who have found a new job this way. The secret is to do this in a thoughtfully researched and highly targeted way rather than sending out a generic letter by bulk email.

The advantages are that there is far less or even no competition from other candidates. You are cheap to hire as no advertising or agency fees are involved and in addition, because there isn't a defined vacancy there is more scope to shape the role in line with what both you and they need.

You are probably going to need to make many approaches before getting a meeting and then several meetings before a job offer materialises. However, this effort and resilience is well worth it as it can be a very successful route to your next job.

Who should you target?

Employers will be more receptive to a proactive approach if you can demonstrate that you are familiar with their type of company and the challenges they face. Perhaps you have worked with similar products and services, have experience working with their suppliers or partners or have lots of knowledge about their target customer base. For instance if you have experience working in sales within the automative industry, then look at any associated company which has a sales function. This might include selling different types of vehicles, automative parts and accessories, new automative technologies, etc

You can gather some target lists by:

- **asking your contacts.** Who do you know that works in an organisation you are interested in? Which organisations have ex-colleagues joined? Ask your contacts for advice on who to target and how to approach the organisations they know, including whether you can mention their name as an introduction.
- **searching on LinkedIn.** Use this to find companies operating in the sector you are interested in; find out who you know that works there and who the hiring manager is likely to be.
- **using directory listings.** Google business listings and websites such as www.yell.com allow you to find local companies, for example type in 'logistics companies Slough'. There are also lots of directory listings for types of companies you can find on the internet, for example www.engineering.com.
- **reading business news.** Trade and local press contain company updates on new contracts, relocations, consolidations and senior management changes. These changes could mean new staff requirements.

Smaller and lower-profile companies are often far more responsive to an approach because they tend to receive fewer speculative approaches and their recruitment processes are less systemised and so more flexible. Widen your target list to companies you may not have heard of.

Making the approach

- **The right person.** Identify exactly who you need to contact within the organisation. It's normally the person who leads the team you are interested in. Check to see if they have a profile on LinkedIn for background information that may help you anticipate their personal style and establish any areas you have in common. Ideally mention the name of a mutual contact who suggested you get in touch.

- **Contact details.** You can usually find out an individual's email address simply by ringing the company and asking for it. Otherwise you can probably guess it by looking at the way other email addresses for the company are formatted. You can also send a message through LinkedIn but it is better to go through the company's communication channel if possible.

- **Email approach.** In your email, introduce yourself, mention your mutual contact if you have one and say why you are contacting them. Include five key bullet points outlining what you have to offer that can make a difference to their company. Use your research on the company to show your understanding of their market and challenges and state why you want to work specifically with their company. You can send your CV if appropriate but your covering letter needs to be sufficiently compelling on its own to grab their attention. Always follow up an email by ringing the manager to whom it was addressed. You might need to ring a few times in order to get through so be prepared to be persistent.

- **Telephone approach.** If you are ringing first rather than writing then you have a very short time to make a good impression so you should prepare a very clear sales pitch that is focused, clued-up on their company, business-like and helpful. You need to outline your background and experience, why you would be an asset to their company and why it's worth setting up a meeting to discuss it further. Then follow-up your conversation with an email providing more information.

- **Handling the meeting.** When you meet, the aim is to understand the manager and organisation's challenges, establish your credibility and build a relationship. You also need to be prepared with ideas about how you might best help them. This might be within a permanent role, a consultancy or project basis but whichever it is you must show how your input directly addresses their needs and can add significant value to their organisation.

- **Follow up.** You will then need to follow up your meeting with an email, usually with a more detailed proposal about how you can work together. If you are lucky you might have just timed it right and they are keen for you to start right away. If not, it's still very important for you to keep in touch. The seeds you have sown at this meeting may well come to fruition at a later date, perhaps when they have the budget to hire you, or internal changes mean there is now a place for you. At that point they may well decide to hire you rather than advertising the role.

Example of speculative email

To: Nita MIrchandani
Subject: Opportunity to work together

Dear Nita

I am writing to you at Graham Smith's suggestion because my extensive background in corporate event management could be very helpful to you in growing this area of your business.

Over the last 10 years I've organized over 150 business conferences and forums for organizations like the CBI, professional services firms like PWC and Grant Thornton, and institutes like the Royal College of Psychiatrists. I am used to designing and organising very high quality and engaging business events achieving capacity attendance and maximum positive PR value for the sponsoring organisations.

This includes:

- *Delivering engaging events that have attracted hard to reach industry influencers such as senior staff from Google and Microsoft who are usually inundated by invitations*
- *Achieving 98% delegate satisfaction rates with consistently high evaluations and regular repeat business*
- *Launching a brand new monthly Round Table event with VIP invitation lists which has been so successful that we have rolled this out to 15 of our other major clients*
- *Creating a highly successful new business networking event for corporate alumni with over 100 senior professionals regularly attending each quarter*
- *Consistently achieving financial targets by meeting ambitious delegate attendance targets and through careful cost control*
- *An extensive contact list of corporate clients, influential speakers, suppliers and venues that I can call upon and with whom I have been able to negotiate preferential rates*

I would be very interested to discuss with you how my experience might be of benefit. I will ring your office next week to arrange a time to talk with you.

Looking forward to speaking with you.

Best wishes

Louis Gabel
Mobile: 07555 555 555

26 NETWORKING

This is one of the most important activities you will need to undertake if you are looking to manage your career. Various research studies estimate that anywhere between 45% and 85% of jobs are filled because the employer knew the person they wanted to hire or the candidate heard about the job through someone they knew. Furthermore, the sociologist Mark Granovetter conducted research which showed that it was often acquaintances or 'weak ties', rather than your immediate network, who were most likely to be helpful to you in your career. This reinforces how important it is that you leave a positive first impression with people you meet and actively try to talk with new people to extend your reach.

Let's look at some ideas on how you can start to build your meaningful network.

Who can I network with?

The answer is everyone. It's not exclusive. However, you have some obvious groups to start with:

- current and ex-colleagues, managers, suppliers, customers, etc
- contacts through professional associations or business groups
- friends, family and neighbours
- community groups in which you are involved, for example faith groups, school, charitable causes
- educational contacts through university alumni, tutors, training courses
- anyone you happen to meet, for example party guests, fellow dog walkers, etc

You might find it helpful to look again at Exercise 22 on page 89 to remind you of your networks.

What will I say?

It's a conversation so start it as you would any other interaction. There might be some pleasantries exchanged and some chitchat as you both talk and listen and find areas of common interest to talk about. The conversation will at some point turn to work – it always does – and at that point, when you have already established a rapport with the person, then you have the opportunity to talk positively about what you do, describe what you are after and perhaps discuss how your conversational partner might help.

- Choose face-to-face over Facebook. The best connections are made in person.
- Ask 'How are you?' not 'Who are you?'. We put far too much stock in job titles and far too little on whether people like the same things as we do.
- Network for the long term. You don't have to 'succeed' at networking, you just have to see where it leads.
- De-clutter your contacts book. Forget being competitive with how many 'friends' or 'followers' you have. Only connect with people who interest, amuse or inspire you.
- And for the timid … shyness in networking is actually the norm. The antidote is to make eye contact, and wait for someone to break the cycle and begin a conversation.

Networking tips from Julia Hobsbawn, Professor in Networking

Interestingly, many people seem embarrassed to talk about themselves in this situation, downplaying what they do and preferring to talk instead about the negative things at work such as their heavy workload or unreasonable boss. It might be enjoyable to have a mutual whingefest about how awful work is, but if your partner walks away none the wiser about what you do and without a particularly positive impression, then this is a wasted opportunity.

Instead, look on this as a potential PR window because you could very well be talking to someone who could help you in your career. If you provide relevant information and are positive and confident about your capabilities, then the chances of them wanting to engage with you further on a professional basis are increased and they are more likely to remember you if an appropriate vacancy comes up.

This is when your 'elevator pitch' needs activating. It's called this because the idea is that in the 30–60 seconds it takes to get in the lift with someone and arrive at your chosen floor you have succinctly conveyed the key messages you want people to understand about you career-wise.

The key components of your elevator pitch are:

- a brief positive overview of your career, for example '10 years working in …'.
- the areas you enjoy, are good at and want to be known for: 'My expertise is in …'.
- a sense of importance about what you do, for example 'Developing policies that help people live healthier lives' or 'Removing logjams to keep everything running smoothly'. If you don't think it's important, why would they?
- any notable successes or name-dropping that will impress, for example 'Built new partnerships with major companies like …'.

Keep the existing conversational tone when you are talking about this so it doesn't suddenly launch into a formal monologue. If you are talking about aspects of your career that you enjoy, you should naturally feel energised and positive and this will come across.

> *'My background is in business improvement and I've run all kinds of interesting projects from restructuring teams and processes for FTSE 100 companies like BP and Barclays to working with exciting tech start-ups who need to develop their infrastructure as they grow. It's about looking creatively and using design thinking to challenge the status quo and anticipate future needs …'*

Your partner may well want to ask you some questions about this especially if you seem very engaged with what you do. If you are looking for a new opportunity be open about this and give them a copy of your business card in case they come across someone who could do with your skills.

Remember that the best way to build rapport is to show genuine interest in the other person, actively listening and being supportive to them. They are far more likely to return the favour. However, if the conversation is not going as you hoped and, let's face it, not every stranger is going to turn into your best friend, then you can always diplomatically extricate yourself by saying it was lovely to meet them but you need to go and mingle, get a drink or you have spotted someone else you need to talk to. People don't expect you to talk with them all evening so it is fine to move on when the conversation has run its course.

What next?

If you have had a pleasant or useful conversation with someone, then suggest you connect on LinkedIn and maybe even meet up again for a coffee if appropriate. Hereafter it may be just an online connection but if you bump into each other again then always take the time to speak with them, even if briefly, so that you continue to reinforce the relationship and leave a positive reputation behind.

27 INTERVIEWS

Fantastic! You have a job interview. They obviously liked your application and they've invited you in to find out more about you. Let's look at how you can convince them that you are the right person for their job.

Preparation

Careful research and preparation are needed beforehand to stand the best chance of success. Your research should include:

1. Going through the job details with a fine toothcomb to make sure you understand the job and what they're after
2. The company's website and social media channels to find out facts and figures about the organisation, its products and services, values and the latest company news
3. A competitor analysis to see how it compares with its rivals
4. Finding out about the company culture by talking to anyone you know who works there. Also check out websites such as www. glassdoor.com where candidates and staff post anonymous reviews of their experiences with the organisation
5. Reading sector reports to find out about wider challenges in the industry. Lots of the big consultancies like PWC, recruitment agencies and sector bodies publish these reports. Just type in keywords into Google to find a selection. E.g. 'sector report telecom'.

This research will give you credibility at the interview when talking about the organisation and help you anticipate the type of questions they might ask and the answers they will be most responsive to. The fact that you have also gone out of your way to diligently research and prepare will also earn you extra brownie points as it will convey your keen interest in the job and your professionalism.

Proving yourself

For every single criteria on their job's personal specification form you must prepare an example to show that you fully meet their requirements. For instance, if they want someone with great negotiation skills then it's not enough just to say that you are a good negotiator, you need to give them specifics such as how often you are required to do this in your job. For example 'I negotiate the terms for about 12 supplier contracts a year', as well as giving them a great illustration of when you did it really well, such as 'The last contract negotiation I managed to achieve a 10% reduction on costs by lengthening the contract term which also gave us the continuity we needed ...'.

Use the achievement statements you built in Exercise 15 on page 73 and the CV guidance in Chapter 22, with a bit of adjustment to match the specific criteria they are asking for.

If there are any criteria where you feel you might not have what they need, then don't ignore it and hope they won't ask – because they will and then you are likely to be wrong-footed. Prepare an answer which shows that any perceived shortfall isn't going to be a problem. You can do this by:

1. Talking about transferable or complementary skills, for example you may not be familiar with a particular database but you have used similar ones in the past.
2. Mentioning other situations where you have been very successful in entering new professional situations and learning quickly, for example having to become an expert in SAP about which you previously knew very little about.
3. Reading up immediately on the area in question or by taking an online course so that you are up to speed (check out www.mooc-list. com for lots of free online courses).
4. Quickly arranging some relevant work experience and talking to someone who can give you the insights you need.

Being realistic about any gaps but showing you have thought about how to minimise them will hopefully impress upon them your keen motivation and adaptability.

Your interview answers

Employers are understandably cautious about who they let into their organisation so sometimes it can feel like they are trying to catch you out with their questions. They will be testing the limits of your knowledge and experience and pushing to find out more about your personality and how you operate in stressful situations. This can sometimes feel uncomfortable but don't take their difficult questions personally, they are just doing their job. Your task is to reassure them that you can do the job and will be professional, motivated and a safe pair of hands at all times.

Some common questions include the following.

- Can you tell me about yourself?
- What do you know about our organisation?
- What experience do you have of …?
- What are your key skills/strengths/achievements?
- Can you describe a conflict situation/failure at work and how you dealt with it?
- Can you give an example of when you have been able to change someone's view?
- What's the most stressful thing you have had to deal with at work?
- Can you tell me about a difficult relationship you had to manage?
- Can you describe the biggest problem or challenge you've faced at work?
- What did you like most/least about your last role?
- What would your last boss/colleagues say about you?
- What did you most/least like about your last boss?
- Why did you leave your last role?
- What motivates you?
- Why do you want this job?
- What are your career goals?
- What are your weaknesses?
- Why should we select you for the job?
- What are your salary/package expectations?
- Are there any questions you would like to ask us?

Your answers to these questions need to be positive, relevant and supported by an example or some other evidence that shows you in a good light. This doesn't mean you should make everything sound as if it was easy. Quite the contrary. Your examples should show there was complexity and challenge involved and it was far from straightforward but despite this you managed to show your mettle and overcome whatever difficulties there were, for example 'I had to deal with a very aggressive customer who I felt was a potential danger to others. I calmed them down by showing I was listening and took down the details of their complaint while alerting security who removed them to a safe area'.

Handling tricky interview questions

Let's look at a selection of the trickier questions that come up with some advice on how to answer them.

Can you tell me about yourself?

This question or something similar such as 'Take me through your CV' usually starts every interview. Don't give a long-winded blow by blow account of your career history or start talking about your personal life. What they actually want to hear is why you are a great candidate for them. Take this early opportunity to make a great first impression. Your answer should:

- talk about your skills, expertise and sector background which are directly relevant to the job
- mention something impressive, for example an award you won or a challenging project you completed
- convey your enthusiasm for the job and the organisation you are being interviewed for
- avoid personal or irrelevant information, for example your children, unrelated jobs or why you are looking to leave your current job.

> ## TIP
>
> Your answer should be about three to five minutes long delivered in a clear, punchy, positive and confident manner.

'I'm a Marketing Director with over 20 years' experience running successful marketing campaigns predominantly in the technology sector. I've had a lot of success with growing business through innovative approaches – for instance last year we grabbed an additional 15% of market share worth £10 million partly by uncovering new audiences. I'm really interested in your products as they have great potential and I know that my track record working in very fast-changing and mature markets could really help you.'

What are your key skills/strengths/or why should we hire you?

Focus on what you know they are looking for from the job details and your research, even if it has been a smaller part of what you have been doing to date. This is what they will be most interested in. Your answer might include:

- technical knowledge, for example IT help desk
- sector experience, for example retail
- job-related skills, for example project management
- management skills, for example people and financial management
- interpersonal skills, for example handling conflict
- personal qualities, for example work ethic

'I bring lots of expertise in IT support and I'm very good at solving issues quickly and efficiently.'

What are your weaknesses?

While many candidates seem bashful about talking about their achievements, they don't seem to have the same reticence about talking about their weaknesses. They often spell out their failings with a relish that is baffling. Others will try and dodge the question by saying they don't have any weaknesses or they revert to a cliché such as 'I'm a perfectionist'. Unfortunately this rather loses its authenticity when the interview panel has heard six other candidates in the same day describe themselves as a 'perfectionist' too.

1. Choose something that doesn't matter for the job, for example map-reading for a job that is based in one location or 'I've got very good Excel skills but I'd like to know more about using pivot tables …'.
2. Identify a 'weakness' that is a positive, for example 'I'm lost without a list. I like to plan everything', especially if the role is very task focused rather than creative and spontaneous.
3. Choose a weakness that you have improved, for example 'I'm a very passionate advocate for our clients but I've learnt that you also need sound economic arguments too so I work very hard to balance the both …'.
4. Use this question as an opportunity to address any doubts you think they might have, for example 'I'm aware that I don't have direct experience of this type of product so I've talked to your sales team and some of your competitors to find out more. I've researched market trends and discussed this with some key people within the sector who've given me their personal view. As a result I feel confident that I can get up to speed in this role very quickly'.

Find an answer which is genuine but which doesn't detract from your suitability for the role and have at least two or three answers prepared in case the interviewer decides to really push you on this.

Why are you looking for a new job?

Do not say (even if it's true) that you just need a job, you want it because it's local or that you are unhappy in your current employment. Never criticise a previous job or employer as it won't play well in the interview. Instead, your answer needs to tell them why you were attracted to apply to this particular job, for example:

- it's a good match between your skills and their requirements
- you are interested in their product/market/sector
- the company's excellent reputation is a draw
- you like the fresh challenge this role offers.

If you were made redundant then it's fine to mention this but keep it short and positive, for example 'I really enjoyed working at my last company but they were downsizing and that meant a number of redundancies including my own role'.

Can you describe a conflict situation or failure you dealt with?

The interviewer is looking for a real-life example to understand more about how you tackle problems, in particular your thinking style, your ability to act under pressure and your interpersonal skills.

Choose an example which shows how you successfully managed a difficult situation, was able to achieve a good result or minimise potential damage and maybe learnt some useful lessons from it.

> 'Had to work in a project group with business partners who all had very different agendas and although I worked very hard to facilitate discussions and find common ground, we weren't making the progress needed. In the end, I suggested that we re-structure the group which meant some difficult conversations but it did finally free us up to get on with the task at hand.'

Avoid talking about any example which was an unhappy experience and which still feels sensitive. Talking about it at interview can easily reawaken those negative feelings and this can easily knock you off balance especially if the interview panel ask you probing questions about it. Choose another example instead.

Tell me about an achievement of which you are proud?

This should ideally be work-related, something that was challenging and where you achieved some kind of positive contribution. For example completing a project where you had to use creativity and problem-solving to make it work.

TIP

You might find it useful to think about positive feedback you have had from your manager in the past about things they feel you have done well.

What are your career goals/career plans?

However you answer this question, you need to reassure them that the job you are applying for is a great complement to your career aspirations, for example 'I'm looking for opportunities to work in a more entrepreneurial team environment which is why I am so interested in this role ...'

Do not talk about career aspirations that could cause the interviewer to doubt your commitment to the role such as 'I want to start my own business' or 'I see this as a stepping stone to working in finance, which is where I really want to be'.

What are your salary expectations?

If the salary is not on the job advertisement, then find out what the salary is before you go to the interview. If the job is through an agency they will be able to tell you the salary range as they will already have established this with the employer so that they can put forward suitable candidates.

Otherwise, you can benchmark salaries by looking at the salary surveys on many of the big recruitment websites or simply type into Google 'salary survey procurement' or whichever type of job you are applying for and it will find lots of sites giving you market information on salaries.

If possible, try to avoid a salary negotiation at the interview to give yourself more room for manoeuvre once you've been offered the job. Unless you have the detail of all of the terms and conditions it is impossible to give a definitive answer anyway. Some useful deflection answers could include 'I'm really interested in this job, so if as I hope you do offer it, then I am sure the salary won't be an issue' or 'Money is important but not the only factor which means I could be looking for anything from X to Y depending on the whole package but I will be happy to discuss if as I hope you offer the job'.

Are there any questions you would like to ask us?

This is a great place to bring in your research. Refer to some recent company news or industry trend you have learnt about and ask the interviewer whether it is likely to have an impact on the job. They will be impressed that you have thought about this. Other questions could include the following.

- What do you think the major challenges for the post-holder are?
- How will success be judged in this role?
- What is it like to work here?

TIP

This is definitely not the time to ask about salary, annual leave, sickness etc. You'll get this information when they offer you the job at which point you can negotiate if you wish to.

Looking the part

Check out the everyday dress code for the organisation in advance. Is it fairly traditional, smart-casual or more fashion-forward? Then aim for a slightly smarter version of what people would normally wear. Everything about your image at that interview needs to be positively working in your favour. You need to look at the top of your game. Invest in a new outfit that makes you look and feel great. Get a haircut and be impeccably groomed. The interview panel are going to be looking at you for an hour and candidates who have clearly made an effort will be judged to be more professional and genuinely motivated to do the job.

Positive mindset

Many candidates worry that talking positively about themselves at interview is somehow bragging. It's not – as long as you support it with some evidence. Remember that employers are not psychic; they will only know what you tell them and if you don't give them the relevant information they need then you are doing both of you a disservice.

Interviewers understand most candidates are nervous so don't worry if your voice seems a little shaky at the start or if you have to ask them to repeat a question. They will be judging your answers against the selection criteria they have established, but also viewing your performance at interview as an indication of your interpersonal skills and how you behave under pressure. Your tone of voice and body language can have a significant impact on their perceptions. If your voice sounds tentative and you seem uncomfortable in your seat then it can diminish your credibility, even if your interview answer is very appropriate. Make sure that your voice can be clearly heard and that your words are underpinned by a strong belief in what you are saying. Have good eye contact with all of your interviewers and smile as though you are genuinely pleased to meet them.

There is so much to consider when you are doing an interview that it is always worth practising out loud and doing a mock interview with a career coach or someone you trust. You need to make sure that your answers are relevant, well-constructed and you are delivering them in as confident a way as possible.

Post-interview

Immediately after the interview send an email thanking the interview panel and saying how you are even more interested in the job. Also feed this back to the recruitment agent if they have been handling the appointment. Your keen motivation can be a tipping point in your favour if there are two equally matched candidates.

The reality is that you will come across some good interviewers and some terrible ones. Some jobs you might get but not others. However, every time you go into an interview room you need to have that positive mindset that conveys your belief that you can do a great job for them and that these are the reasons why.

If you are not successful, especially if it was for an organisation you really wanted to work for, then ask for feedback and write them a charming thank you email saying how much you enjoyed meeting with them and how you would love to be considered for any further opportunities. You may or may not get any meaningful feedback but people will remember how you handled the rejection and your keen motivation to still work for the company. People remember these gestures. Given that an estimated 20% of new appointees fail to pass their probation (Spring Personnel Survey 2014), it's well worth keeping this relationship warm as they might need you later.

28 BE YOUR OWN BOSS

According to the Federation of Small Business, small businesses accounted for 99.3% of all private sector businesses in the UK at the start of 2016 and 76% of those businesses did not employ anyone aside from the owner. According to the The McKinsey Global Institute, 162 million people in Europe and the US, up to 30% of the working age population, are engaged in some form of independent work.

It looks like this trend will accelerate as new technologies mean organisations need less core staff. Companies are predicted to increase their use of freelancers or outsource work to smaller companies for specific projects or contingency situations.

This growing freelancing trend is part of what is now often called the gig economy. Working for both corporate clients and private customers it can range from professional services such as consultancy, counselling or home tutoring, to project work like building a website or carrying out tasks such as courier services and gardening.

The rise of new online marketplaces such as AirBnb, Etsy and Uber are also significantly changing the marketplace as they enable freelancers to directly sell their wares and access potential sales leads from customers without the need for an old-style organisational middleman.

Self-employment is great if you want to have more freedom in how and when you work. However there is less financial security and you are always looking for your next assignment, so you have to be comfortable being in constant audition mode. There are many people, and I include myself in this, who feel that starting their own business was a great decision. But it definitely has its challenges.

Here are some pointers if you are thinking of working freelance or setting up your own business.

- **Financial viability**. You need hard-headed commercial savviness. Think carefully about your investment, including set-up costs such as legal fees, websites and marketing as well as any on-going overheads like premises, equipment, stock and accountant fees. Write down your earning needs and projected costs so you know how much work you need to generate each month and how much to charge in order to make a living. You also need to consider the length of your sales cycle to ensure that you have sufficient cash to see you through those cash-burning early months or even years so that you survive long enough to start seeing profits.
- **Risk temperament**. Setting up a business takes substantial investment and there is never guaranteed income, so you have to be comfortable with the level of risk you have taken on. Even established businesses can have lean months so it's not for the faint-hearted.
- **Prepare to be hands on**. It's not just going to be about delivering the work to the customer – that's the easy bit. You're also going to need to be chief salesperson, office manager, financier, IT fixer and general 'jack of all trades' as you no longer have an organisation taking care of these things for you. You are unlikely to be an expert in all of these things so do what you can and get help where you need it.
- **Regulations**. As a business-owner you have serious compliance responsibilities including legal obligations, health and safety, regulatory requirements, HMRC tax returns and employment law. You will need to get to grips with all of these.
- **Be niche**. Be clear about what you are good at and market your services directly to your target customer rather than trying to be all things to all people. This way you can build a reputation for excellence rather than diluting your expertise. People are also more likely to find you this way as they will use keywords for particular services when they are looking online.
- **Check out your competition**. See what the competition is offering and how you might compare. You need a good answer to a customer who asks why they should choose you rather than the company around the block. Find a positive differentiation to attract them – whether it is your expertise, lower costs, personal service, fast turnaround, local connections – whatever is true and is likely to resonate with the customers you are trying to impress.
- **Sales pitch**. You will need to be a good salesperson because if you don't get potential customers to commit to hiring you then you don't have a business. If this is a new area for you then get some sales and marketing training so you can convert those discussions into sales.
- **Go online**. Create a website, LinkedIn and Google+ profile and a company page for Facebook and Twitter which show off what you can do and how you do it, along with great testimonials from people who think your work is fantastic. It's no time to be modest! Be careful that any of your more personal social media profiles don't detract from your professional messages.

- **Don't sell your services and products too cheaply**. Your prices and fee structure should reflect market rates but also remember that you now have overheads in a way you didn't as an employee. There will be set up costs such as equipment and legal fees, increased utility bills if you are working from home and on-going costs including your time spent winning new customers and running the business. You also won't get sickness or annual leave entitlements so build some contingency funding into your rates.
- **Use your network**. Who do you know that could use your services? Make sure professional contacts, family and friends all know what you do and can recommend you. It's important that you go out and meet with new people to spread the word so look for business forums where you can talk with people who might have a need for your services.
- **Keep connected**. It can be lonely when you are between freelance jobs or if the nature of your work means that you tend to work from home. Build time into your working day to meet with people. Lots of freelancers choose to work from a coffee shop instead just so they feel less isolated.
- **Time management**. Be realistic about the time it will take you to complete a project so that your fees properly reflect the amount of work you do. Also be careful about boundaries as organisations can sometimes assume that you're on call for seven days a week when actually your arrangement is for a specific number of hours or weeks. If the organisation is transgressing this then either manage their expectations about your availability or seek to renegotiate the contract to give more flexibility.
- **Learning curve**. If this is the first time you have run your own business then prepare for a steep learning curve as you encounter lots of things for the first time, from pricing your services, to creating your marketing, to your first sales meetings. You'll make mistakes, everyone does, but you'll learn from them.

Do the side hustle

It's a growing feature for not just freelancers but also employees to have another revenue stream or passion project besides their key professional role. This might be renting space on Airbnb, creating jewellery, copy-writing, website design or running a charity social enterprise. The additional income can be a welcome boost and insurance should anything happen to your main job. It can also be a way to make your working week more interesting and help you develop skills that you may want to use more full-time in the future.

If you would like to set up your own business then it also worth looking at franchises as these provide a more supported way to start your own business under the umbrella of an established brand. They provide advice and training as well as brand marketing in return for an upfront investment and ongoing franchise fees. You can check out www.thebfa.org for more information.

Top tips for freelancers

Plan your new business pipeline. Where are you going to get clients from? Most of your work at the beginning will come from emailing friends, family and people in your existing network. But you need a plan past that, whether it's through social media, paid ads, local business networks or referrals from clients happy with your work.

Don't sell yourself short. You'll be competing with lots of other freelancers and will need to convince business owners that you're the best person for the job. Make the most of your assets and present the best version of yourself you can (without exaggerating too much!).

Structure your day. There's nothing worse than working from home and not having a structure to your day. Multiple visits to the kitchen or cleaning the house becomes much more tempting! Because there's no one looking over your shoulder, plan your day appropriately: what tasks are you going to tackle and when? And plan a time to stop as well. You don't want the working day to drag on into the evening.

Ben Matthews, author of **Freelance in 30 Days,** *www.benrmatthews.com*

PART 8

Advice for dealing with tricky career challenges

This section offers practical advice on dealing with some tricky career challenges, along with success stories from individuals who have made positive changes in their career.

In this section we will:

- manage career 'skeletons' so they don't scare off the recruiter

- look at tips for changing career

- discuss issues around redundancy

- confront being overqualified or feeling too old for a job

- discuss workplace stress

- address challenges for recent graduates and school-leavers

- hear some career change success stories

29 CAREER SKELETONS!

While your career may have been a blaze of nonstop glory, most people's careers have had ups and downs. Periods of unemployment, unreasonable bosses, overwhelming workloads or health issues are likely to affect most of us at some point in our career, but they can put you on the defensive with recruiters who will naturally be asking you all kinds of detailed questions about your career history. So here are some tips to ensure those career skeletons don't scare off the recruiter.

Factual accuracy

As a candidate you are of course presenting the very best version of yourself. However never be tempted to tell a lie. All factual data such as employment dates, qualifications, grades, etc, must be accurate. Recruiters will be validating your application by checking your CV is consistent with your LinkedIn profile, by taking up references and carrying out checks on your qualifications and previous employment dates. If a lie is discovered you will immediately lose trust and you could potentially be prosecuted for fraud.

> ## TIP
>
> Do not be tempted to lie: 324 people were prosecuted in 2013 in the UK for fraudulent employment applications. This has a maximum prison sentence of 10 years under the Fraud Act 2006.

Baggage-handling

If there is a career issue you feel is sensitive, then be careful to control your verbal and body language when you talk about it to prospective employers.

Individuals often start giving far too much detail about it in order to justify themselves. At interview you can see them reliving past wrongs or mistakes and becoming quite emotional. The personal baggage on display is often more off-putting for the employer than the issue itself. Resist the temptation to talk about it at all, or, if you have to, keep it short, tightly scripted and upbeat.

Lessons learnt

Everyone makes mistakes – the idea is to learn from them. If you have to talk about a career failure, acknowledge there were difficulties, avoid criticising individuals or the company and frame it as a useful if painful learning experience. Perhaps this made you realise that you were better suited to roles where you could use your front-facing people skills rather than back office, or that you prefer working in SMEs rather than big corporates. Just make sure that whatever you say you are looking for more of, this is consistent with the role you are applying for.

References

If you left on less than happy terms with your last employer then check out what will be on your reference so you know how much to declare to a new prospective employer. Some employers will only provide confirmation that you worked there and your dates of employment. If not, try and get an agreed reference from your organisation, especially if you have signed a settlement agreement. Otherwise wait until the job offer stage before releasing your referee details and arrange for them to contact people who you know will be happy to give you a positive personal reference. Adopt the 'baggage-handling' and 'lessons learnt' strategies if you need to explain why your manager is not giving you a good reference.

Career gaps

Most people will have career gaps at some point in their career, whether it is for family reasons, travelling or a period of unemployment. If you are currently on a break, then you are going to need to reassure the employer that your skills and knowledge are sharp and you are professionally 'match-fit'. The best way to do this is by acquiring recent experience, whether it is voluntary work, some paid or unpaid consultancy work, sitting on a committee, helping with community activities or going on a course. This is especially important if your break has been longer than six months.

Use a functional CV (see page 213) to aggregate all of your skills and experience on the first page of your CV so a recruiter won't actually see your employment dates until the second page, by which time you have hopefully already persuaded them that you are worth considering. You can also minimise the appearance of gaps by using years rather than dates for your employment history, for example '2016–2017' instead of 'July 2016–Jan 2017'. Where you have a number of jobs that didn't last very long you could also group them together as '2015–2017 worked in a number of temporary contract roles in retail and manufacturing companies' rather than emphasising just how long you spent in each.

Health/disability issues

The Equality Act 2010 means that employers can't ask about your health or your sickness record until after they have offered you the job. They are also expected to make reasonable adjustments to accommodate those with a disability, which is defined as any physical or mental impairment that has a 'substantial' and 'long-term' negative effect on the ability to do normal daily activities.

Candidates are often unsure whether to disclose sensitive health information to a prospective employer. If it is likely to have little or no effect on your future working life then you don't need to share it, either on your CV or at interview although you might choose to share it in any confidential occupational health questionnaire you are asked to complete once the job offer has been made.

However, if your disability is such that you are likely to need special arrangements during the recruitment process and in the job, such as access to a disabled parking space, then it makes sense to signal this in advance so the employer is prepared and can help you. As for any candidate, it is important that you focus on what makes you a great person for the job rather than letting yourself be defined by your health condition.

> ## TIP
>
> See www.gov.uk/rights-disabled-person for more information on your rights.

Disappointing academic results

Not everyone is academic or does themselves justice in their exams. Academic results become less important as your work experience builds and you undertake more vocational training. However, a surprising number of candidates seem compelled to draw attention to their disappointing results on their CV. It's much better to downplay them or even leave them off all together. For instance if you got a third class degree then write this as BSc Biology without any reference to the grade, or group together '5 GCSE passes' rather than itemising their low grades.

Do make sure your CV shows you have attended lots of training activities so employers can see that you are keen on continuous learning even if you were not academic. You could even consider courses as a mature student or the free massive open online courses (moocs) available through www.openuniversity.com.

Ex-offenders

Over 15% of the population in the UK have a criminal record whether this is a fine, conviction or a custodial sentence. If a prospective employer doesn't ask about any convictions then you are under no obligation to tell them. Under the Rehabilitation of Offenders Act 1974 most convictions and cautions become spent after a specified period of time which means that you would not need to declare these either. There are some exceptions such as roles within the NHS or working with children. Check out www.nacro.org.uk for full information.

30 TIPS FOR CAREER CHANGERS

Changing careers is a substantial undertaking. It's not just about changing jobs, it's about creating a new professional identity. This requires significant learning and adaption, and the ability to persuade others to see us as we now want to be seen. Here are some tips to help.

- **Reality-check.** Research the types of jobs you are interested in by checking out adverts and job descriptions, as well as talking to agencies and people who work in this field. Find out the everyday nitty-gritty of what the job involves before you decide to make the move.
- **Role models.** Find mentors and role models who can be a touchstone for you to focus your efforts, chart your progress and benchmark your professional evolution. This will help keep you on track and provide a sounding board for any interesting diversions or tricky challenges.
- **Tackle any gaps.** You will have a number of transferable skills that you can bring forward to your new career but you will also need to develop new skills and knowledge, undertake training and arrange work experience either on a paid or unpaid basis. Consider stepping stone roles or side projects if you can't move into your new career right away. These will help you build up the new credentials needed.
- **Career evolution.** We saw in Part 2 that your career hasn't just happened overnight. Changing your career won't be instantaneous either. It can sometimes take years, during which time you are continually experimenting, creating new learning opportunities, discovering more about your new field and then gradually carving out a new niche for yourself within this. Enjoy the journey.

> Resist the temptation to start by making a big decision that will change everything in one fell swoop. Use a strategy of small wins, in which incremental gains lead you to more profound changes in the basic assumptions that define your work and life. Accept the crooked path.
>
> *Hermina Ibarra,* **Working Identity: Unconventional Strategies for Reinventing Your Career**

- **Reassure employers.** Prospective employers tend to be wary about career changers. They may be concerned about your lack of experience, your motives or your commitment to your new career. Counter this by positioning your career change as a natural progression as you discovered more about the things you were good at and enjoyed. Focus on your transferable skills and try to show how even in unrelated roles, the seeds of your new career were already present.
- **Chronology.** When talking to employers, focus on your suitability for this new role rather than talking about your previous career first. Use a functional CV that uses the first page to outline your relevant skills and experience and put your employment history on the second page.
- **Inside track.** Aim to come across as someone who is 'in the know' rather than a novice. Make sure you are up to speed with the challenges and trends in your new sector including how technology, impending regulation or political changes might impact on the role.
- **Be proactive in your job search.** Don't rely only on advertised posts as you are likely to be competing with other candidates with far more experience than you. Instead focus on networking and contacting employers directly to offer your services. Temporary work can also be a great route into organisations you are interested in.
- **Action plan.** It's easy to get distracted so a structured project management approach to your career change is more likely to reap results than erratic fits and starts. It doesn't mean this has to be rigid; your plan always needs to be open to change, but giving yourself targets and tasks can keep your energies focused. See Part 9 for your Career Action Plan.

31 FACING REDUNDANCY

Redundancy ranks as one of the most stressful of life experiences for many people. Here are some tips to help you with the practical and emotional challenges it can bring.

Depersonalise

It can be easy to take your redundancy personally and to feel aggrieved either by the decision or by the process leading up to it. However, try to maintain a civil relationship with the company wherever possible, even if you disagree over the manner of your exit. You will still need a reference for your next job and your paths may cross again in the future. When talking to prospective employers about your redundancy, present it as having been a tough business decision for your ex-employer but don't criticise the company or particular individuals.

Know your rights and negotiate

Check out the exit terms and notice periods in your contract as well as any in-house redundancy policy. You may also want to talk to your trade union or an employment lawyer to make sure that due process is being followed and you receive everything that you are entitled to. The ACAS website is very helpful for information on this: www.acas.org.uk.

Always ask for more than your employer is initially prepared to give, whether it is an enhanced lump sum, extending your leaving date or keeping the company laptop. If you are working with an employment lawyer then they can also negotiate on your behalf. See www.personalcareermanagement.com/settlement-agreements for more advice on negotiating settlement agreements.

Outplacement

Many companies will pay for outplacement support so it is always worth asking for this as part of your redundancy package. This is where a career coaching company such as Personal Career Management will help staff who have been made redundant to find another job. If this is provided for you via the company there are tax advantages for you, and the company will pay the VAT, making it substantially cheaper than if you tried to purchase career coaching services privately.

Brush up your employability

Assess whether there are any gaps in your experience or training that could be a barrier to getting another job and address them. It's a great time to take some of those courses you have always been too busy to go on as not only will this enhance your skills, it will also impress employers with your commitment to continuous professional development. There are many courses you can study for online alongside looking for a new job.

Plan your finances and think positive

Calculate your financial situation so that you have a realistic picture of your finances and cash flow. Finding a new job can sometimes take a few months, especially if you are looking for a more senior role so it's wise to be careful with the finances. Contact the Jobcentre to find out your entitlements.

Redundancy can be very unsettling. All of your stress management strategies are likely to be needed here, whether it is stepping up the exercise, yoga or mindfulness, keeping connected with other people, or making time to do something you really enjoy such as playing football or volunteering.

> ## TIP
>
> See pages 264–266 for tips on stress management.

32 HELP! I'M OVERQUALIFIED

There might be lots of reasons why you've applied for a job where you have over and above the skills and experience required. You might think this would make you a great catch for the employer. So why does this rarely work – and what, if anything, can you do about it?

Do you really want this job?

If you've been applying for more junior roles, then before you try to persuade an employer, be honest with yourself first. You may need a job but is this really the job you want? If you are ambivalent about this, no matter how much you try, then your uncertainty is going to show through. Your covering letter and CV is likely to be unfocused and half-hearted and your body language at interview is likely to be saying very clearly 'I'm not sure if I want this job' even if your words are saying the opposite.

Employers understandably want someone who is highly motivated and who is going to stay in the role. Why would they hire you if they suspect, probably quite rightly, that you would be looking for another job within the month?

Positive choice

If this more junior job is one that you genuinely need and want, then you must convince the employer that your application is far from a second-best career choice. Otherwise they may wonder whether you are only applying to them through desperation because you struggled with the demands of working at a more senior level or there has been some other career distress that has provoked your intended downshift.

Even if any of these are true, always be careful about sharing negative reasons for applying for a job because they can raise additional concerns. For instance, if you say that you want a job with less responsibility then the interviewer might wonder whether there were any performance issues in your last job. Even if you are down-shifting to a more junior part-time job for family reasons or pre-retirement be careful that you don't come across at interview as half-hearted or a clock-watcher. Find a positive reason why you are attracted to the job such as wanting to get back to the more customer-focused activities you enjoyed, which your previous role had taken you away from.

The right pitch

If you are looking for a more junior role as a way to get your foot in the door of a new career path then remember the employer's priority is someone who can do the job, not to do you a favour. Don't dumb down your previous jobs, but select relevant content for your CV and interview answers that are pitched at the right level. For instance, if you are going for a sales job rather than a sales manager role, then focus on the sales you have brought in personally, the accounts you've won and pitches you have made, rather than talking about the results of the team you manage.

To downplay your seniority you could try using a functional CV rather than an historical one with all of your relevant capabilities on the first page and your career history relegated to the second page. This allows you to highlight your transferable skills and experience, and attach less importance to your more senior track record. You could also put your higher level qualifications at the back of your CV or even leave them off if you think they are disadvantaging you.

Entry routes

Use your networks as you can probably be more honest with them about what you are looking for next and why, and they may be able to help shape a flexible role which meets your needs. Temping is another great way to get into organisations you are interested in as there seems to be less of an issue in hiring more senior staff in junior temporary roles. Once you are there, you can make connections, check out any internal vacancies and try and position yourself for future opportunities from the inside.

33 AM I TOO OLD?

We're all living and working longer and it's estimated that by the mid–2030s people aged 50 and over will comprise more than half of the UK adult population. However, despite this, some mature candidates worry about being viewed as 'past it' by employers. As with any job application, first and foremost you have to prove you can do a great job for the employer. However, here are some other tips to counter any potential negative preconceptions about older workers.

- Take off your date of birth from your CV and dates of early education. Consider a functional CV rather than a chronological one so that your employment dates are on the second page (see page 219). You don't need to include all of your work history if it goes back a long way. Your early career history can be omitted or roles grouped together.
- Employers don't want someone who will just coast in the job. Talk about being motivated to do the job and work for that particular organisation so that you counter any pre-conception that you might just be looking for any job to eke out your pre-retirement.
- Talk about recent professional achievements rather than glories from the past to emphasise that you are still professionally focused.
- Show energy and drive by using positive action words in your CV and at interview, such as 'created, initiated, developed …' and pay attention to your physical fitness and posture to reinforce the impression that there is plenty of life and sparkle left.
- Make sure you are bang up to date with technology and developments in your field by talking about training courses, conferences, reading, trends and news coverage. This will show that you are genuinely interested, committed to continuous learning and up to speed with current challenges.
- Emphasise your adaptability and flexibility with examples of where you have been involved in organisational changes and how you contributed to its implementation, for example learning new processes

following the introduction of new industry regulations.

- You have to be digitally savvy. If it's a while since you looked for a job you may not have needed to contend with social media for instance. Read Chapters 23 and 24 to make sure you are visible online.
- Look the part at interview and also in your LinkedIn photo. It's not a beauty contest but you need to look contemporary, not old-fashioned. It might be time for a new interview outfit and haircut.
- If the interviewer is much younger than you then be careful not to fall into a parent/child type of interaction or one where you become the boss mentoring a junior protégé. Keep an adult to adult relationship dynamic, one where you are supportive and helpful without being patronising.
- If there has been clear evidence of age discrimination, then you can always pursue a legal claim if you wish. See www.acas.org.uk for more information.

34 DEALING WITH WORKPLACE STRESS

Now, of course, work is always stressful to some degree. There is never enough time in the day, you might not have the resources you need and people can be difficult. Organisations also have a habit of decanting their systemic failings onto the staff, who may try valiantly to mop up the mess, but who can end up feeling overwhelmed. Here are some practical steps to help.

Spot the early warning signs

When you are at home do you seem to spend a lot of time worrying and brooding about work? Maybe it's keeping you awake at nights or work is a relentless topic of conversation with loved ones. Stress at work can also find physical expression in terms of backache, panic attacks, migraines, everlasting colds, etc. It is often easier for others to spot that this is more than just 'a tough week at work', so if people are telling you that you 'don't seem to be yourself', it's time to pay attention.

Deal with the symptoms of the stress

You may just need some time away from the workplace to refresh, reinvigorate and get some much needed perspective that there is indeed life outside of work. So book that holiday, mini-break or sabbatical. Start reclaiming your lunch breaks and finishing work on time. Go to the gym, learn mindfulness, buy some positive self-help books or write a journal where you can vent your feelings. Your career resilience will definitely be helped if you work on keeping yourself physically and psychologically in good shape.

Talk to your boss

It can be hard to be objective when you are in a horrible work situation, but try to put your emotion to one side, and think about what the real work issues are and what could be done practically to help alleviate the difficulty. Then go and discuss this with your boss in a calm, rational and professional manner. Sometimes, just expressing whatever it is that is causing you the most stress can be amazingly cathartic; sharing the problem rather than shouldering the entire burden. If you can't do the work you've been asked to do, remember that it is your boss's problem too, and they need to know so they can do something about it before it all potentially goes belly-up. They also have a duty of care towards you so if they want to avoid any stress-related injury or constructive dismissal claims at a tribunal, they need to show that they have listened to you, acted in a fair way and made reasonable adjustments where they can.

If your problem is your boss, then you may need to talk to someone else in your organisation, perhaps HR, another manager you trust or an employee representative. They can advise you on how you might best deal with this.

Psychological support

If you are feeling overwhelmed and miserable and you have felt like this for a while, then it's worth talking to your GP or a counsellor. The website www.mind.org.uk is a great information resource with lots of advice on psychological well-being. Also check out whether your organisation has an Employee Assistance Programme which is a confidential service designed to help staff with any personal problems, from well-being issues to advice on practical matters such as finances, family care, housing, etc.

There are always options

If it becomes clear that the employer is either unwilling or unable to make the changes that would make a difference to you in your job, then there are always options. You could stay and fight, perhaps raising a grievance, getting advice from an employment lawyer, career coach or your trade union if the organisation seems unwilling to shift. You could also look at whether there are other roles in the organisation that might work better for you. Otherwise, it may be time to start looking for another job.

Individuals tend to put up with far more than they should in horrible work situations, hoping that it will get better of its own accord. Sometimes it will. Usually it doesn't. When you start to do something about it, whether it is talking to the boss, seeking advice and support, or brushing up your CV and applying for other jobs, you will immediately start to feel better because you have started to take back control, rather than feeling powerless. Every job will have its ups and downs, but life is too short to spend it in a job where you are unhappy or where the personal cost is too high.

35 RECENT GRADUATES AND SCHOOL-LEAVERS

Your early career is a time for learning and experimentation so even if you think you know exactly what you want to do, your plans might change. Work out what it is you actually enjoy or don't like by trying out different things. Undertake internships or do some voluntary work or temp jobs in different types of organisations. If there are a number of options that interest you, then go and talk to individuals working in those fields to find out more. There is so much information online about different careers, career resources available via professional bodies and job details to look at via recruitment sites. See Part 5 for more information on how to research your options.

What are employers looking for?

While there are differences between roles, employers tend to look for the following skills and personality traits when they are hiring first-jobbers.

Communication/social skills
IT/technical
Organisational
Emotional intelligence
Team-working
Customer focus
Analytical

Creativity, innovation, initiative
Quality awareness
Problem-solving
Commercial awareness
Resilience
Fast-learner
Hard-working

They will be interested to see if you can demonstrate that you either have a natural aptitude for these, or that you can quickly develop them.

Use your work experience

Your work experience may be limited but in your applications you need to make the most of all the experiences you have had. This includes any experience at all in a professional environment whether it has been paid or unpaid, whether it was for a single day or a whole summer. For instance, if you have worked in a shop or in a sales-related role then you can show that you understand customer service, can work to targets and know how to represent a brand. If you worked in a café then you can show that you are used to working under pressure, problem-solving, and following health and safety and financial procedures. Always be working in some capacity while you are looking for a job so that you have current professional experiences to talk about and to show your work ethic.

Extra-curricular activities

Don't forget about any other positions of responsibility or projects you have been involved with, such as being a student representative, running a university society or participating in entrepreneurial ventures or artistic endeavours. You can use these to demonstrate your leadership potential, organisational abilities or creativity. Voluntary activities such as fundraising, youth work or conservation projects can be used to show your energy, work ethic and community spirit; all attributes that suggest to the employer that you will be a good team player.

CV and applications

These need to be tailored to each job and organisation. For instance, if you have been working in a mobile phone shop and are interested in applying for a marketing role for a particular technology firm, then you could describe yourself in the profile on your CV as follows:

'Business graduate with excellent retail experience who enjoys working in highly customer focused sales environments. Acquired in-depth product knowledge which meant that I could quickly advise customers on the best solutions to match their needs. Consistently achieved personal sales targets and actively helped others in the team to meet theirs. Interested in using my insights from this front-line sales experience to further a career within a marketing function of a technology company like ABC.'

However, if instead you wanted to apply for an accountancy role, you could use the same work experience to highlight different relevant skills, for example:

'Business graduate used to dealing with cost calculations, payment processes and complying with strict financial procedures as a result of my experience working in retail sales for a mobile phone store. Enjoyed advising

customers on the different cost models and the plan which would work best for them given their needs and budget. Interested to use these financial and analytical business skills to further a career in accountancy.'

You can see from the above, the same experience is used to convey different skills in line with what is most likely to be of interest to the employer. This is far more effective than just writing on your CV, 'worked in a mobile phone store'. Itemise all of your relevant paid and unpaid work experiences in your applications, drawing out their relevance to the role you are applying for.

Include details of all your course modules only if it is vocationally related to the job such as a social work degree, or there are other relevant areas to the job you are applying for, for example a module on politics if you want to work in the civil service. Also draw out elements from your course such as data analysis, original research, group project work, creativity and presentations along with your software skills as these are all directly transferable to the workplace.

You can include hobbies and interests but make sure they are genuine and be careful about what they say about you. Base jumping might give cause for alarm for a corporate role but maybe not if you are applying to work as an outward bound teacher.

TIP

See pages 217–218 for an example of a graduate CV.

No room for error, on paper or digitally

The employer is judging not only the content of your CV or application but the way you go about applying for the role. Your application needs to be impeccably well presented with a covering letter to show your professionalism. Ask someone else to check your application before it is sent, to weed out any errors or clumsy phrasing. Errors in your CV are the fastest way to end up in the reject pile as the employer will assume rightly or wrongly that you have poor attention to detail and lack the conscientiousness to produce work of good quality.

Keep your professional and personal online life separate. Make sure your privacy settings are tight on your personal social media pages and that there is nothing a potential employer can find out about you online that may give them pause for thought.

Graduate schemes/entry-level jobs

The graduate entry schemes are usually massively oversubscribed as are the new professional apprenticeship schemes for school-leavers run by organisations such as the BBC. You will have an advantage if you have excellent grades, already have good work experience either with that organisation or similar, and you can demonstrate a genuine commitment and interest to working with them.

It is also worth remembering that most graduates do not enter the workplace via a graduate scheme as they account for a very small proportion of the amount of jobs available. You might have more success by contacting the organisations directly for other entry level or temp jobs and then applying to the graduate entry scheme or the departments you are interested in once you are already inside. Ninety-nine percent of private companies in the UK are SMEs (small- and medium-sized enterprises) and, while they might not have a graduate scheme, they can offer great experience especially as smaller organisations are often more flexible in their job design.

Be proactive

In this digital age, the phone has become one of the most underutilised resources in job searching. If you haven't heard from a potential employer, ring them up. Always be charming! Ask about the progress of your application but also use the opportunity to express your interest in the organisation and the job. Sometimes by taking the initiative to ring up, you are already standing out from all the other candidates. I remember talking to the hiring manager of a very prestigious organisation that received piles of applications from Oxbridge graduates. He would simply wait to see which applicant would bother to ring up and then invite only those for interview.

You should also try different methods of contacting employers. Network wherever you can, bringing in favours from family and friends. Write to those people you want to work for directly. Use Twitter and LinkedIn to follow and have dialogue with companies and individuals who you are interested in working for. You won't get a response every time but the more energy you put into this the more likely you will find an opening. This initiative is precisely the kind of quality that employers look for in their new recruits.

36 CAREER CHANGE SUCCESS STORIES

As inspiration, here are some stories of people who have successfully made positive changes in their career. They share their insights about the things that helped them.

CASE STUDY

TREVOR

I had spent 12 years working for a company and had become increasingly unhappy in the organisation. The owner of the business was approaching retirement and they didn't want to invest in the company, in fact they were taking money out, and this was making my job very difficult indeed. It was very demotivating and I was worried that the sector was declining and I would be left in a dying industry. I was very stressed. I knew I had to get out but I had no idea what my next step should be. I toyed with lots of ideas, from opening a bar abroad to working in a new role in a completely different industry. However, when I sat down to flush out what I really wanted and to look at all of my ideas, it came out that actually, I really enjoyed my sector, I knew an awful lot about it, had great connections and I was very good at it. There were lots of business opportunities in the sector, I was just demoralised because my current organisation wasn't good at capitalising on them and I knew that this was unlikely to change as I had already tried. This gave me confidence that there was scope in my field but I needed to approach it differently. I decided to negotiate an exit agreement with my boss and then set up my own business instead. I've now worked with lots of my old contacts and the business has gone from strength to strength. It's infinitely more rewarding and I feel so much happier and in control. My advice would be that you don't have to make a complete career change to transform your career. Maybe you just need to work in a different way.

LUCY

I had worked in the media sector for 12 years but new global trends meant different organisational needs and values and it made me start to think about what career pathway would be fulfilling for me. Teasing out the values and passions that I hold and mapping them to my skill set and career background has been really helpful. Also thinking about how I can contribute to a business or organisation whilst achieving my personal goals. I found I wanted to work within the same sector but in a different industry. I have moved roles twice and each time have been able to deploy skills, knowledge and contacts in a different, arguably better way than before. It's meant a far more interesting career for me and I have felt so much happier and this has had a knock on effect on those around me especially as the way I work now suits my lifestyle. Yes, I sought advice on my CV, applications, cover letters and the practical stuff in order to get those jobs, but for me it was the deep reflection about my values and my skills that helped me understand what I needed to do to help them find expression at work – and this is what has made the difference to my sense of career satisfaction.

TOM

I got my first job because a friend worked there and got me an introduction. It never really felt like me. There wasn't one particular moment when I thought I wanted to move, but I started realizing that I was in my 30s and I couldn't go on doing this job much longer or it would be too late to do something different. My friends were all doing really well and I was getting quite despondent about my life choices. I had started off by thinking about completely different careers but when I took a step back and thought about the things I loved, my love of writing came out. I wished I had studied English at university and in my spare time, I write for a sports website so there was some background to writing but I certainly didn't think I could make a career out of it. A job came up at work to be a copywriter. I didn't think I stood a chance as I had no experience but applied and it was no surprise when I didn't get an interview. But I went back and asked what I could do to improve my chances next time round. As a result of my query, the copywriting department gave me a writing test. They really liked what I wrote and I got the job. It was only because I went back to them with particular questions that I was given the opportunity to reapply, in effect, by doing the writing test. Seems really simple but so important. Now I write everything from advertorials to investigative copy for national papers, and I love it! I get to do the research, come up with an angle, build the picture and then write the piece. It is really worth getting to grips with your career because the pleasure you get from finding something you really like is amazing.

SUSAN

CASE STUDY

I was a Senior Manager with an excellent salary and a large team of people working for me. I liked my job but I had been toying with the idea of working for myself since I had twins. I wanted a stimulating career which paid the bills, but I also wanted to spend quality time with the boys. The leap away from a very successful and worthwhile career with a high salary to working from home for myself, with no certainties about income or future success, was a huge one. However, I took the plunge and became a management consultant. Even though I had left my employer full of excitement about my next move, I still felt a bit like a wounded wildebeest at first. One moment you are part of a pack where your role is highly valued and the next, even though you decide to go, you're on the edges of that family. In some ways it did feel almost like a bereavement. I'd stress the importance of building good relationships and not burning bridges because my previous employer has been really helpful in opening doors for me. I've found other people very helpful as sounding boards, advice and support. I've also built myself a virtual team with some national partnerships and local community work because otherwise there would be some days when I wouldn't be talking to anyone – you replace one sort of team with another. What's been great for me is that this career change has enabled me to continue working in a sector I loved while balancing the family's needs and that's exactly what I needed.

MARY

CASE STUDY

I had a job I adored as Director of Human Resources at a very prestigious organisation. I had won awards and so had my team for the great work we had been doing. After 10 brilliant years, a new Chief Executive came in with new ideas about the organisation and my role was made redundant. When you are made redundant, however valued you know you are at your organisation, you do find your confidence is dented and I felt hurt. I was also concerned about being over 50 and how people would perceive me in the job market. This was the first time since I was 19 that I'd had the chance to stop work and have a really good think about what I wanted to do next. I used this book and worked with a career coach to help identify my skills and the areas I wanted to work in and they helped me with my job search preparation too. This helped build my confidence again and it also became clear that for me the job I was after was not necessarily for a big organisation like last time, but a smaller more informal organisation where I had a wider business remit. My new job is in the third sector involved in building sustainable communities. There are lots of challenges, I am never bored and the culture is great. Much more informal than I was used to previously and this has been a real positive. My number one tip – don't go rushing in to look for another job. I know a number of people who've rushed headlong into getting another job and it has proved to be a mistake Take the gift of time to really look at yourself and more importantly, what you want to do for the next stage of your career as this ensures that you apply for the right jobs for you and you are more likely to be successful.

CASE STUDY

ANDY

I had completed my PGCE straight after university and I enjoyed my training but did find working in the schools very difficult. It felt like most of the staff, including me, were demotivated and given the hours we all had to work I wasn't surprised. We all spent most evenings working. It was exhausting and when our first baby came along I just realised that I couldn't continue working at the same pace – I needed some down-time. I then had to think about what else I could do. The aspect that had drawn me to teaching the most was actually helping people to learn, this was something that I enjoyed so I wondered if I could do anything else connected with learning. I talked to lots of ex-teachers to see where they had gone. I investigated lots of different learning and training role possibilities from corporate training, to being a home tutor, to devising educational materials and software. In the end it was a casual suggestion from a friend of mine that I talk to his wife as she worked for a training company, and this led to my new career. They ran a lot of apprentice training contracts and personal effectiveness workshops for youth charities so having a trainer who was an ex-teacher and used to dealing with young people and creating learning programmes was ideal. I still feel that I am using my expertise but I don't have the same pressures that I did as a teacher which I think would have made me very ill if I had stayed there much longer. My advice is to do something about your career when you feel unhappy rather than sit there and be miserable. And talk to people about your ideas because I found people had some great suggestions that I hadn't thought of and it did turn up a job for me.

PART 9

Your career framework

We've been on a long journey of self-discovery throughout this book and it's now time to capture all of your career insights and translate them into practical actions. This section will help you chart exactly what you need to do to achieve your career goals and provide a sturdy framework for future career decisions.

In this section we will:

- create a Career Action Plan with clear goals and a schedule of practical tasks

- produce a summary Career Insights Guide for future reference

- share your final reflections and write a message to yourself

37 CAREER ACTION PLAN

You may know exactly what you need to do to progress your career, and in fact have already taken the first steps. If so, fantastic!

However, your career is not something that you fix overnight or even in a couple of weeks. It can be very easy to become distracted, let other things take priority, or become derailed if things don't happen as quickly as you had hoped.

This is where a written action plan can really help. First, writing down your goals makes them tangible and clear, rather than remaining as a vaguely expressed notion at the back of your head.

Second, your Career Action Plan will guide you as to what to do and when, outlining the steps you need to take in order to achieve your goals. You can then plan this into your diary rather than relying on spontaneous bursts of action as and when you remember.

Your Career Action Plan will be constantly evolving and need to be regularly reviewed but at least if you have a plan, you know where you are heading and how to get there.

EXERCISE 44

YOUR CAREER GOALS

We are going to start your Career Action Plan using a mind-map exercise as in the following example. The aim here is to generate lots of ideas that we can use to write a more formal action plan.

Let's use this model to start thinking about your career campaign.

1. In the central circle on page 279, write your key career objective. This may be an immediate need or a longer-term aspiration, and it should be as clear and direct as possible. You may want to review Exercise 40 on page 165 where you identified your career decision as well as other exercises such as Exercise 3, the Work/life balance assessment on page 17, Exercise 7, I want ..., on page 30) and Exercise 31, Visualising the future, page 118.
2. In the outer circles, identify the intermediate career goals that will help you achieve your overall career objective. Examples might include:
    - personal development goals – such as acquiring the technical knowledge you need
    - bridging skill or experience gaps – such as taking on voluntary work for those returning to work after a break
    - making changes in your current role – such as improving your job satisfaction
    - tackling the external job market – such as getting shortlisted for the jobs you want
    - personal goals – such as work/life balance.
3. Add as many of your career goals as you can to the diagram, aiming for a minimum of four. You may want to look back to the action points section in your reflections exercises at the end of each part of the book to ensure you don't miss anything.
4. Once you have entered your career goals, write down all the practical tasks you need to undertake to help you achieve each goal. Add as many suggestions as you can to the above diagram, with each task branching off from the relevant aim. You should have a minimum of five tasks per goal, but add as many as you can. You can always edit them down later.

TIP

Transfer your mind-map onto a separate piece of paper if you need more room.

EXAMPLE

The central circle is your overall career objective/aspiration. The outer circles represent the intermediate career goals that will contribute towards helping achieve this bigger goal. Each of the outer circles then branches into the tasks that need to be undertaken to achieve each specific career goal.

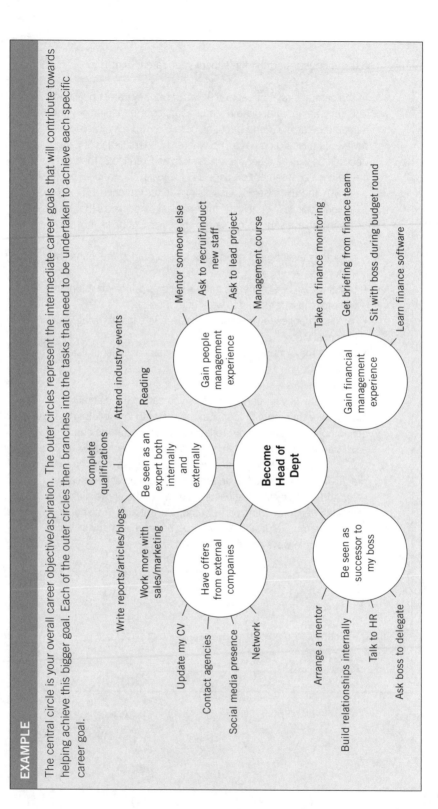

Career Action Plan mind-map

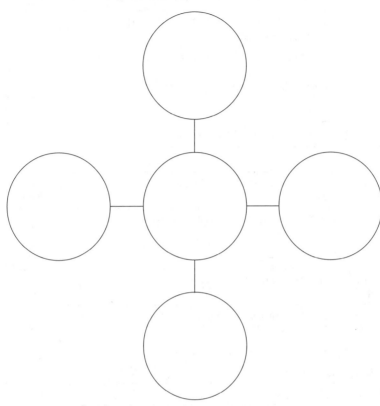

Below are some ideas for tasks as prompts to help you.

Ideas for your Career Action Plan

Getting organised	
Get the computer equipment, software, internet access I need	☐
Ensure my mobile voicemail works and message is appropriate	☐
Allocate a set time/day I will work on my career goals/plan	☐
Create document to track job applications or conversations with recruiters	☐
Use an electronic or paper calendar to remind me of my career tasks	☐
Preparing for the job market (see Part 8 for advice)	
Devise CV(s)	☐

Get independent feedback to make sure CV is effective	☐
Read about different job search strategies, for example adverts, agencies, direct approaches	☐
Develop my 'elevator pitch' to introduce myself to strangers	☐
Practise my interview skills and get some feedback	☐
Rehearse telephone calls to recruiters	☐
Buy an interview outfit, get a haircut, update my look	☐
Organise business cards	☐
Contact recruitment agencies and headhunters and post my CV(s) online	☐
Apply for a target number of jobs each week/month	☐
Proactively contact a target number of companies each week/month	☐
Arrange a target number of networking meetings each week/ month	☐
Read local paper/journals to identify companies that may need my skills	☐
Use my grapevine to keep eyes and ears open	☐
Using social media	
Join LinkedIn	☐
Ensure privacy settings are set on Facebook account	☐
Link with interesting companies and participate in their online communities	☐
Use Twitter to help my job search (see page 223)	☐
Seek out other online professional forums for interacting with fellow professionals, information sharing	☐
Follow @changecareer and @corinnemills on Twitter for career tips and advice	☐
Increase visibility in my field	
Write articles, media commentary or blogs on my subject or specialist area	☐
Train others, become a lecturer, speak at conferences	☐
Set up a website to display examples of my work	☐
Join relevant professional associations or forums and attend events	☐
Volunteer for a committee role	☐

Career development with my current employer	
Talk to my manager, HR and decision-makers within the organisation	☐
Ask for feedback	☐
Join a cross-organisational project group	☐
Volunteer to write a report	☐
Organise a charity event	☐
Arrange a mentor	☐
Ask to attend conferences	☐
Apply for internal vacancies	☐
Join cross-organisational working groups	☐
Meet for lunch with other colleagues	☐
Ask for additional responsibilities	☐
Ask for flexible working or reduced hours	☐
Arrange work experience in another department	☐
Ask for a secondment or a sabbatical	☐
Ask for a pay rise	☐
Personal and professional development	
Keep up to date with developments in my field, for example new software or legal changes	☐
Investigate training courses, conferences, workshops	☐
Study for a qualification	☐
Create a written learning log to capture and reflect on key learning challenges	☐
Join or create a group of fellow learners, for example an action learning set or peer supervision group	☐
Read relevant books and journals	☐
Work with a career coach	☐
Upgrade my professional memberships	☐
Undertake voluntary work to extend my skills and experience	☐
Self-employment (see pages 247–250 for advice)	
Research different self-employment options	☐
Investigate franchises	☐
Conduct customer and market research	☐

Create a business plan	☐
Review finances and investment	☐
Develop marketing materials	☐
Talk to an accountant and the bank	☐
Personal	
Talk to my partner about my career goals and how they can help	☐
Enlist support of family and friends	☐
Ensure quality personal time for self and family	☐
Get healthy by taking exercise and watching diet	☐
Build confidence through self-help books, counselling or courses	☐
Improve social life	☐

Your mind-map on page 279 should now be bursting with ideas about practical things you can do to achieve your career goals.

Be SMART

The next stage of your Career Action Plan is to organise these ideas into a schedule.

You may have heard of the SMART rules for goal-setting and how helpful they can be when devising personal and business-related goals. The SMART rules remind us that if our goal-setting it is to be workable, it must be:

- **S**pecific: It is important to be detailed and precise. If there is any vagueness, this is an indicator of a stumbling block ahead and it needs addressing.
- **M**easurable: Identify success criteria so that you can determine whether or not you have achieved your aims. For instance, instead of saying you will network, set yourself a target of how many networking meetings you will have in a month.
- **A**chievable: Ensure you are realistic. Make sure your goals are stretching but doable. Ambitious goals should be broken into smaller, more achievable steps.
- **R**elevant: Everything in your Career Action Plan should be relevant to your overall career objectives. Keep it focused.
- **T**ime-bound: Set target dates and deadlines for the goals and tasks to keep momentum and avoid procrastination.

Using the SMART criteria and your answers to Exercise 44, we are now going to write down a task list.

YOUR CAREER ACTION TASK LIST

1. Write down each of your career goals and how you will know when you have achieved it, for example by completing a qualification or being invited to an interview.

2. List the relevant tasks you will undertake for each career goal with a date for completion.

3. For ongoing tasks, such as reading a professional journal, give yourself a target for how many times you will do that task per week or month.

My career goals

CAREER GOAL 1

Tasks/activities

CAREER GOAL 2

Tasks/activities

CAREER GOAL 3

Tasks/activities

CAREER GOAL 4

Tasks/activities

EXAMPLE

CAREER GOAL 1

For my expertise to be sought out both internally and externally.

I will know I've achieved this when the management team start asking me directly for advice and I am asked to give presentations internally and at industry events and I am invited onto project groups and to sales meetings.

Tasks/activities

- *Ask immediately if I can accompany the sales team as the in-house technical expert.*
- *Complete my postgraduate qualification in 2019.*
- *Attend conferences and speaker events at least three times a year and get to know the organising committee(s).*
- *Read my industry journal every month and subscribe to newsletters on industry topics.*
- *Become a volunteer committee member for my professional association at AGM in April.*
- *Offer to write a report on industry trends and distribute it to the managers by June.*
- *Find a project group that I can get involved with by March.*
- *Represent my boss at least once in the next year at one of the cross-industry functions.*

CAREER GOAL 2

When my boss retires, for me to be considered as the natural successor. *I want to be offered his job when he leaves next year.*

Tasks/activities

- *Ask my manager at appraisal meeting in March if they can delegate more tasks/responsibilities to help my development.*
- *Make sure that from now on when I do reports for senior management team they are aware that I have produced them.*
- *Develop strong working relationships with other departments in coming year so that I become their main liaison person. Aim to visit all six departments by end of year.*
- *Arrange an external mentor for advice about making the move to more senior level by end of year.*
- *Talk to HR before February so that they know my career objectives.*
- *Talk to my boss's boss in the coming year.*

Manjit

Now that you have a clear list of what you are going to do to achieve each goal, let's organise your tasks in date order so that you can integrate these activities into your diary. This is a good opportunity for you to double-check that you are being realistic in terms of your time schedule.

TIP

Things can often take longer than you think, so be generous with the amount of time you allocate: but once you have finalised your schedule, always do your best to keep to it.

EXERCISE 46

YOUR CAREER ACTION SCHEDULE

1. Add real dates to the following schedule so you know the actual calendar date for the completion of each task.

2. Review your task list and group the tasks in date order so that you can see clearly on a calendar what you are going to do when.

3. Complete the following schedule. An example is given on page 288.

What will I do tomorrow?

What will I do by the end of next week?

What will I do by the end of the month?

What will I do by the end of three months?

What will I do in six months?

Within a year, I will …

What will I have done within three to five years?

EXAMPLE

Tomorrow (01/11/2017) I will …

- *see if there is any help available for women returners at my local job centre.*

By the end of next week (14/11/2017) I will …

- *find out about local colleges providing IT skills courses*
- *organise a personal email address*
- *change my voicemail message so it doesn't have the kids on it.*

By the end of the month (30/11/2017) I will …

- *speak to the office at the school to find out about any job vacancies there*
- *offer to help brother-in-law with some of his admin to get experience*
- *investigate after-school childcare and costs*
- *talk to my friend Carol who runs a recruitment agency.*

By the end of three months (31/01/2018) I will …

- *start doing some voluntary work so I have experience to put on my CV*
- *contact my old boss and some of my work colleagues*
- *have developed a CV that I can send out for jobs*
- *be looking at the local paper for jobs.*

Within six months (30/04/2018) I will …

- *be applying for jobs with my new CV – at least one a week*
- *develop a covering letter I can adapt for different jobs*
- *learn how to apply for jobs online*
- *learn how to do a LinkedIn profile*
- *do some interview skills training to build confidence.*

Within a year (31/10/2018) I will …

- *be working in a part-time job or in a voluntary role which will help me get paid employment*
- *have all my IT skills up to date*
- *feel much more confident about going back to work because I have gained some practical work experience*
- *investigate teacher training courses and also other career options for potential retraining.*

Within three to five years (31/10/2022) I will have …

- *maybe done a teacher training course or other course*
- *investigated possibilities for setting up my own business from home.*

Jo

> I found writing my Career Action Plan quite challenging. However, it was because I had planned in the routine stuff, targeting myself for four good networking meetings a month, that I heard about the job from Ian. I might not have spoken to him otherwise.
>
> **Rob**

Well done! You have now created your Career Action Plan, so you know exactly what you need to do and when. Whether you use a paper diary or a calendar that is integrated with your computer software or phone, make sure you schedule in the above activities.

TIP

Make sure your plan is highly visible and accessible, and provides you with regular reminders about your goals and target dates. It's worth integrating this with the calendar on your computer and mobile.

Progress review

You may find that your career goals and objectives start to change as you progress through the year. There may be changes of plan: for instance, you might have secured your new job more quickly than you thought; or the threat of redundancy may give you a new sense of urgency.

If this is the case, just amend your plan accordingly, but don't, whatever you do, let it lapse. Review your plan after six months to check progress and include any new career priorities.

It is also recommended that you complete all three career action planning exercises afresh each year. Make a note of the progress you made during the past year, and then reappraise your career goals and the career activities needed for the year ahead. Some elements may remain the same, but you may be quite surprised at how much has changed, especially if you have been making good progress with your plan.

Rewards and celebrations

Whether you have achieved one of your main career goals or simply plucked up the courage to do something positive which took you out of your comfort zone, you should reward yourself.

If it is a major achievement, such as the new job you wanted – celebrate. Go out for dinner, have a party, go to the pub! Announce the news on your LinkedIn and Twitter profiles. Notify people who have helped you and the trade press, if appropriate, especially if you want to grab the attention of recruiters or potential employers for the future.

You should also reward yourself for anything you have achieved that was personally very challenging. For instance, if you are a nervous networker, but successfully spoke to two complete strangers at an event, this is worthy of a well-deserved pat on the back too.

Well done! You now have a Career Action Plan to help you move your career forward in your chosen direction.

38 YOUR CAREER SUMMARY

The career coaching process has offered a very in-depth analysis of your career and the way ahead. In this penultimate chapter we bring together your key insights and findings from the whole book as a useful reference document for the future. Also included is a final reflections exercise and an opportunity to write a message to yourself for the future.

EXERCISE 47

MY CAREER INSIGHTS DOCUMENT

My career capital

1. Review Exercises 14–23 to record here the main elements of your career capital and what you have to offer a prospective employer. These could include the following.
    - Your key skills (Exercise 14, page 67)
    - Your achievements (Exercise 15, page 73)
    - The value you add to a company (Exercise 16, page 79)
    - Your professional credibility (Exercise 17, page 82)
    - The training you have undertaken (Exercise 18, page 84)
    - The knowledge you possess (Exercise 19, page 85)
    - Any additional work experience or voluntary work (Exercise 20 page 87)
    - Relevant interests and information (Exercises 21, page 88, and 23, page 90)
    - Your network (Exercise 22, page 89).

2. Note the key points of what makes up your career capital below.

My personal strengths

1. Identify from your career history examples of positive behaviours such as resilience, hard work and relationship building (Exercise 12, page 58).

2. Look at Exercises 25–27 (pages 97–104), which examined your workstyle. Pick out your positive traits and the organisational contexts which would best suit you.

3. Review the positive feedback you received from others in Exercise 28 (page 107).

Blocks and bridges

1. Review Exercise 42 on page 183 where we looked at career blocks that could be holding you back.

2. What are the things that might get in the way of your career progress?

3. How will you overcome them? Look back at the advice in Chapter 18 to help you.

What might get in the way	What will help

MESSAGE TO MYSELF

Imagine yourself in a year's time. If you could talk to yourself from the future and give your present-day self some advice, what would you say? What positive words of advice and encouragement can you offer? What pep talk can you give?

> *It is not the mountain we conquer but ourselves.*
>
> **Edmund Hillary**

Make this message to yourself as heartfelt as you can. You could include any of the following.

- Why your career goals are important to you.
- What difference would achieving your goals make to you or others?
- Advice on how to overcome any anticipated obstacles.
- Words of encouragement and confidence-building.
- Addressing any fears or concerns.
- Reminding yourself of the support you have around you.
- Focus on your capabilities and strengths.

FINAL REFLECTIONS

For the last time, make a note of your reflections and any thoughts or ideas that have surfaced during this career coaching process. You may want to revisit the reflections exercises at the end of each section to help you bring together what you have learned. This might include the following.

- What have you learned?
- What, if anything, has changed?
- What might you do differently in the future?
- Where is there work still to be done?
- Any other comments.

TIP

See Exercises 8 (page 32), 13 (page 62), 24 (page 91), 29 (page 112) and 41 (page 166) for your past reflections exercises.

39 AND FINALLY ...

I hope that you have found this book helpful, thought provoking and of practical use. Its key message is that to achieve a rewarding career you need to do more than just work hard in your job. You have to proactively **manage** your career and this takes thought, research and lots of action.

This becomes even more important in a fast-changing workplace, where jobs are rapidly changing and people are working for longer. Your clarity about what is right for you career-wise and your ability to refresh and reinvent your career will be a huge advantage in maximising your job satisfaction and enhancing your employability.

I hope that this book has also opened up some new career possibilities for you to consider. Whatever your circumstances, there are always options, whether you want to stay within your current organisation, move to a new company, change career direction or start your own business. Your career development is in your own hands!

We may be coming to the end of this book and the career coaching process, but your career will be a continuing story rather than a closed chapter. I hope that this book has laid the foundations for an exciting new career adventure. It is over to you from here!

I wish you every success.

Corinne Mills

If you would like to share your story of how this book has helped you, we would love to hear from you.

Email us at info@personalcareermanagement.com.

Career coaching

If you have enjoyed working through this book, you may be interested in some real-life career coaching.

Personal Career Management, which was founded by Corinne Mills, offers specialist career coaching and outplacement services both on a one-to-one basis, via Skype and through their online portal. Its team of coaches helps with career analysis, option appraisal and planning as well as providing advice and support on all aspects of job hunting including CVs, interviews, networking and using social media. It also provides market intelligence and research services.

Its coaching clients are drawn from a wide range of occupations and industry sectors, both from the UK and abroad. Many of them are seeking to explore their career options, change sector or role, or improve their job hunting success. Personal Career Management also works with corporate clients ranging from FTSE 100 companies to charities, public sector organisations and SMEs.

The company is career expert for *The Guardian*, Telegraph Jobs, Trinity Mirror, CV-Library, Monster and for several professional institutes, and also frequently appears on BBC television and radio, Sky News, CNN and in the national press advising on career-related issues.

You can find out more about its services via the Personal Career Management website which also contains many useful free career resources including articles, career tips and videos on career-related topics.

Contact us on:

Website: www.personalcareermanagement.com

Email: info@personalcareermanagement.com

Telephone: +44 (0) 1753 888 995

Facebook: www.facebook.com/careermanagement

Twitter: @changecareer @corinnemills

You can find downloads for selected exercises from this book at www.personalcareermanagement.com/careercoach.